ask
discover
live smart

100 answers to 100 questions

about being a

Great Dad

100 answers to 100 questions

ask · discover · live smart

about being a

Great Dad

Christian
LIFE
A STRANG COMPANY

Most CHRISTIAN LIFE products are available at special quantity discounts for bulk purchase for sales promotions, premiums, fund-raising, and educational needs. For details, write Christian Life, 600 Rinehart Road, Lake Mary, Florida 32746, or telephone (407) 333-0600.

100 Answers to 100 Questions About Being a Great Dad

Published by Christian Life
A Strang Company
600 Rinehart Road
Lake Mary, Florida 32746

www.strang.com

Cover design by Whisner Design Group, Tulsa, Oklahoma

ISBN 10: 1-59979-478-0

ISBN 13: 978-1-59979-478-5

BISAC Category: Religion/Christian Life/General

First Edition

08 09 10 11 12—9 8 7 6 5 4 3 2 1

Printed in the United States of America

As the family goes, so goes the nation and so goes the whole world in which we live.

Pope John Paul II

C o n t e n t s

Creating a Legacy of Godly Wisdom in Your Kids

Navigating Adolescence

The Power of Family Traditions

Being a Dad to an Adult

Introduction

There's nothing quite like being a dad. From those first moments you hold your sons or daughters in the delivery room to the day you sit proudly as they receive those high school diplomas certifying the world thinks they are ready to face it on their own, fatherhood is the most important—and possibly the most joyful—responsibility of your life that you were *never* trained for!

Even though you may feel like it sometimes, you are not alone. Even though the TV dads of today are nothing like the ones you grew up watching, the time-honored truths of being a great dad really haven't changed. Sure, there are new technologies and such to deal with, but the age-old principles of wisdom still apply. The most important thing is to be open to learning, and by picking up this book, you have made a good start.

The questions that follow will help you explore how to keep your kids healthy and happy as well as help you be the father and life coach that raising kids today demands. The old adage "The acorn doesn't fall far from the tree" still holds true today. Here's to your becoming a solid oak that your kids can depend upon and will look to for wisdom and courage when they need it most.

> *Turn the hearts of the fathers to the children.*
> Luke 1:17, NKJV
>
> *A child does owe his father a debt, if dad, having gotten him into this peck of trouble [life], takes off his coat and buckles down to the job of showing his son how best to crash through it.*
> Clarence Budington Kelland

1 question

What exactly do dads do?

The image of what makes a great dad has changed significantly in the past five decades. The ideal of Ward Cleaver has changed to the lovable bumbling of Tim "The Tool Man" Taylor. As the perception of the role of a dad has changed, how has it affected the responsibilities of being a father? What does being a great dad look like on a day-to-day basis? What challenges do you need to be prepared for?

answer

Perhaps the most reassuring news is this: despite changing times, standards, and attitudes, the role of being a dad really hasn't changed. Regardless of cultural attitudes or entertainment's portrayals of today's family man, a father still has critical responsibilities. These include being leader of the home, providing for his family, protecting his wife and children from an at times dangerous world, teaching kids to be responsible adults, and building legacies of a happy home life that will lay a foundation for the homes where his grandchildren will grow up.

The way people perceive all that, however, has probably changed the most. Fathers may no longer be called kings of their castles, but they are still leaders of their homes.

Men still need the foresight to prepare today for whatever tomorrow will probably bring. Dads don't decree; they direct. Fathers are more like chief executive officers managing corporations than monarchs anymore, and, truthfully, that change is for the best. Being CEOs demands better communication and more initiative as family leaders. Fathers inspire and motivate families to draw together to learn how to make good decisions.

While there may be a million things that seem to be against a father's success, the fact is that each man has within him the power to master himself to do what is right and be a godly example to his family—and that is still the most important key to being a great dad. It all starts with you.

worth thinking about

▶ **Great dads** are visionaries. Put down on paper where you would like your family to be when your kids graduate from high school.

▶ **Your children** and family are greatly influenced by who you are as a person as well as how you lead. What kind of a man do you want to be as their example?

▶ **As the father** is the head of the family, so the wife is the heart. Get together regularly with your wife to evaluate how you are doing as a dad.

> *Fathers, do not exasperate your children; instead, bring them up in the training and instruction of the Lord.*
> Ephesians 6:4, NIV

question

What are your roles as a dad?

So, where do you start? Maybe you just found out you are about to become a dad, or perhaps you already have kids in high school. What can you do today to become the great dad you want them to look to when they need help most? What areas of your life do you need to improve? What areas are you doing well in? What "hats" do you need to keep handy to slip on as needed?

answer

Fatherhood isn't for the faint of heart, and no one becomes a father knowing what he is getting into. Fathers grow as dads in the same way their children are growing as human beings—the trick is staying one step ahead.

Dads are responsible for the physical basics of provision and protection (meaning to protect both your kids from the world and the world from your kids!) as well as the social and spiritual needs of their families. Dads are responsible for helping their kids find a purpose in life, grow toward a career, and develop as healthy individuals able to stand on their own and give to those around them. As such, dads are not just providers, financial planners, in-home law enforcers, and household security but also teachers and counselors, coaches and physicians, therapists and pastors, advocates and guardians, listening ears and sentencing judges.

Being a great dad can be a lot like spinning plates on sticks—you have many different things going at once, and if you don't pay careful attention to each, something is going to crash to the ground and shatter. The key is balance—keeping each area (plate) in proper balance as well as keeping yourself balanced enough to pay attention to each area as needed. You are the leader in making sure your home is a place of joy, peace, patience, grace for one another, honesty and integrity, fairness, humility, and self-control. As you develop these traits and live them before your family, your kids will emulate and build them into their characters as well.

worth thinking about

▶ **What do you use** as a planner? A calendar, a pocket computer, or a daily appointment book? Do you keep family goals as well as business plans in it?

▶ **Dads have primarily** six worlds that they operate in regularly: spiritual, mental, social, physical, financial, and family. Do you have plans for growth in each of these?

▶ **Your inner strength** of character to do the right thing comes from your relationship with God. Make sure you have daily time to build and develop that relationship.

> Let me be weighed on honest scales,
> that God may know my integrity.
> Job 31:6, NKJV

3

question

What does a great dad look like?

Our culture today is fiercely independent. Families tend to live far away from grandparents and aunts and uncles, and mentoring is all but a dead art. So where do you find examples of what a great dad should look like? Do you have a role model? Do you know other men who have successfully trod this path and are thus able to forewarn you of the pitfalls and prepare you for the times ahead?

answer

There are many great men today, but few great fathers. The qualities that make a great public figure are not necessarily those that make a great dad. As a young father you are caught between the need for guides—those who have gone before you and know this fathering territory—and the need to be strong in yourself—independent, self-sufficient, and competent. Young men long for mentors but are also resistant to what they will receive in them. It is hard to go to other people, lay your life before them, and let them evaluate how you are doing living this life, and so men tend to avoid seeking advice from older men, even if they respect them. It is a catch-22 that leaves dads vulnerable to major mistakes while the answer could well be sitting in the pew next to them.

Many families are fatherless today not just because fathers run out on their families, but because young fathers also avoid finding older father figures to mentor them into what being a dad is really about.

Dad, whether you are young or older, you need to actively seek out role models and learn from them. Sure, there are a ton of books, like this one, on being a dad, but they won't replace finding great dads in your community who can show you the ins and outs of the road you are heading down. Chances are, they know some things that can help you along the way, if you are just humble enough to ask.

worth thinking about

▶ Look for other dads who have strong relationships with their teenagers. If their relationships with their kids are strong in that chaotic period of life, you need to know what they know.

▶ What is your relationship with your father like? Is he someone you would look to as a mentor? Why or why not? What about your father-in-law?

▶ Men have much more of a tendency to be isolated than women do. As a dad you need a support group of others who are going through what you are and have also made all the mistakes themselves.

> A guy . . . who has a resistance to authority is begging to be useless. What I mean is, he isn't receiving any advice on how to live, and in turn he isn't able to hand advice down to those who are coming behind him. And if he is handing down advice, it isn't good advice. I mean it isn't tested and tried by years of experience.
> Donald Miller

question

Do you need help
being a father?

Men tend to be independent—dreaming of being the solitary hero blazing new frontiers and thinking thoughts no one has ever considered before. Is that a key to being a great dad, though? Is there something instinctual about it—something men are born with—or is it something men have to learn? Where should you go for the help you need to become the dad you feel called to be?

answer

From the beginning, it was God's design that all kids should be double-teamed. That is why it takes a man and a woman to make a child, why marriage is a holy enterprise, and why the family unit is the primary building block of all societies. Beyond that, God has also organized His people into local churches so that they can work together to spread His ways and His blessings. While being a great dad is based primarily on each father's decision to do continually what is right for his kids, the design was never intended for you to be alone in doing it.

First of all, dads need to be accountable to other dads. You need to have fathers you respect to whom you can go for advice and look to as role models. Second, you need other leaders in your community to reinforce stability in your children. A significant compilation of research indicates that kids grow up more healthy and resilient to setbacks and self-destructive behavior if they have three to five adults in addition to their parents they can confide in. These could be babysitters, teachers, coaches, Sunday school teachers, club leaders, and so forth.

While fathers have the helm, it takes a crew to sail the ship, and that crew—beginning with your wife—is hand-picked by you. Yes, you need help to be a great dad—and God has provided that help from your neighbors to those sitting next to you in church. Make sure good people who share your values surround your children and help you be the great dad you want to be.

worth thinking about

▶ **Is there a men's group** at your church where you can freely discuss fatherhood issues as part of your accountability to God and your family? If not, you should start one.

▶ **There are already organizations** in your community, from Scouting to youth groups, that are looking to help kids grow up to be healthy, contributing adults. Find out how to plug into one.

▶ **As you find out** about youth organizations and sign up for them, volunteer to help out as well. Such groups always need adults of strong character.

> All mankind is of one author, and is one volume. . . . No man is an island, entire of itself . . . because I am involved in mankind; and therefore never send to know for whom the bell tolls; it tolls for thee.
>
> John Donne

question

What if your dad wasn't so great?

Family patterns often repeat themselves. Research shows that abusive fathers tend to have had abusive fathers themselves, and family backgrounds can affect everything from alcoholism to economic status for generations. What if your family history is one that you don't want to see passed on to your kids and grandkids? What if your father isn't a role model for the type of dad you want to be?

answer

Never underestimate how much your father will affect the father you become. Whether you want to admit it or not, even though your likes and dislikes may be very different, as well as skills and talents, most of your unconscious habits in dealing with others have been ingrained into you by your father. You cannot be a different father than your father was just by wishing it so. You need to become aware of your own behavior and habits and find ways to change them into those of the great dad you aspire to be.

But it is not about cutting ties with your past as much as it is blazing your own future. You need to be brutally honest with yourself and find friends who will help you get where you want to go. James likened reading the Bible to looking in a mirror because through reading the Bible regularly, God can show you how He sees you. He shows you what parts of your character to build upon and which to prune away. It will help you put on the attributes of Jesus and break bad or unhealthy patterns in your life.

There is really only one remedy to the self-defeating patterns of your past: replace them with good habits and attributes such as the fruit of the Spirit—love, joy, peace, patience, kindness, goodness, faithfulness, gentleness, and self-control. Build such characteristics into your life, and you can replace the pains of your past with dependability and inner strength.

worth thinking about

▶ Every dad has his good and bad traits. What are some of the positive traits you inherited from your father that you would like to see passed on?

▶ Pick out some areas or characteristics where you feel you need to grow as a person. Remember, you will grow in increments—don't expect change overnight.

▶ Love covers a multitude of sins—that is how grace works. Are you overflowing with grace, or are frustrations making you bitter? If you fill yourself with God's love, slights and insults can take no root in you.

> *You may wonder why a son isn't punished for the sins of his father. It is because the son does what is right and obeys my laws.*
> Ezekiel 18:19, CEV

Why are church and local community service important?

I don't know what your destiny will be, but one thing I do know: the only ones among you who will be really happy are those who have sought and found how to serve.

Albert Schweitzer

6

Are you the man you want your son to become?

Dads like to share their interests with their sons—they buy them a baseball glove or a fishing pole before they can even walk. While you dream of what you will do together with your son, do you also consider who you will become together? Character, as well as skills, is built through doing things together—and as the saying goes, it tends to be caught more than taught. Are you modeling the man you want your son to become?

answer

Though it is far from a perfect analogy, have you ever tried to train a dog? If you have, you learn fairly soon that you can't really train a dog; you can only train yourself. If you discipline yourself to act in certain ways, your dog will learn to react in certain ways. You learn to make your dog behave by doing certain things. However, if you never attend training school with your dog, you don't know how to act, and your dog will reflect that confusion. Dogs respond to what you say only by learning to respond to what you do.

In a similar way, training sons in character isn't about training sons—it is about training yourself. Kids learn to react before they begin to decide things for themselves and turn those decisions into behavior. In a pinch, do your kids respond with the truth when a lie can get them out of trouble? Do they act unselfishly even though it is not in their own interests? Do they exercise self-control and choose to put off play until their work is done? Do they choose to help Mom with something before plopping down in front of the TV? You can't plant lemons and get oranges.

worth thinking about

▶ Jesus often taught in parables because stories give character legs, faces, and voices. Do you have family stories you can tell your kids to show the importance of having integrity?

▶ First things first. On your way home each night, plan to do something with your kids before you sit down to relax.

▶ You have to learn self-control before you can instill it in your children; you have to be a man of character before you will see character in your kids. Plan who you will be first.

> Until you have a son of your own . . . you will never know the joy, the love beyond feeling that resonates in the heart of a father as he looks upon his son. You will never know the sense of honor that makes a man want to be more than he is and to pass something good and hopeful into the hands of his son. And you will never know the heartbreak of the fathers who are haunted by the personal demons that keep them from being the men they want their sons to be.
>
> Kent Nerburn

question

Are you the type of man your daughter should marry?

For better or for worse, daughters tend to marry men who are like their fathers. Their concepts of how they should be treated by the opposite sex are built upon how they were treated as a blossoming woman. Their communication patterns with other men will be built upon how they learned to talk with you. Are you helping your daughter become a princess or a pauper in her own eyes?

answer

It is hard to quantify the relationship between a father and his daughter. It is much more than hugs and tickles and rainbows as they grow older. Daughters learn self-respect from their fathers more than their mothers. It is through their fathers that daughters learn the line between dependence and independence. It is through their dads that they get a sense that their world is a safe place to explore, as well as a safe place to be feminine. They also learn how they should be treated by boys at school through observing how their dads treat their moms at home.

Studies have shown that girls who don't have fathers in their home or don't receive affection from their dads will look for that tenderness from other male figures—generally the boys they meet at school. Somehow God wrote it into their DNA that they need a father's love, just as sons need a nurturing mother to keep their aggression within proper parameters. Girls also learn that they deserve to be treated with respect when their fathers treat them respectfully.

Daughters grow up to be doctors and lawyers as well as housewives, to be civic leaders as well as PTA volunteers. As a dad, are you building into your daughter the confidence and can-do attitude to achieve whatever God has put in her heart? Treasure her as the gift from God that she is.

worth thinking about

▶ **Show your daughter** the courtesies you would like her to expect when she is someday dating. Hold the door for her, take her coat, seat her at the table.

▶ **Listen to your daughter** and learn about her world. Just as with your wife, there are times she just needs you to listen and not just give her answers.

▶ **Don't be afraid** to share your interests with your daughter even if they are things girls aren't usually interested in. There is nothing wrong with a girl who can score a baseball game or put a worm on a hook.

> *Certain is it that there is no kind of affection so purely angelic as of a father to a daughter. In love to our wives there is desire; to our sons, ambition; but to our daughters there is something which there are no words to express.*
>
> Joseph Addison

8

question

How do you balance work, home, and play?

Life doesn't get any less complicated as you grow older. In high school, you learned to balance activities with homework; in college, much more homework and even more activities; when you got married, work, marriage, and hanging with the guys; and now you have kids! At each stage you felt you had just a little more than you could handle, then in the next you looked back at all the free time you had before! How do you keep it all in balance?

answer

There is no question about it—dads need to be organized. Plus no one ever looks back over his life and says, "Man, I wish I had spent more time at the office and less time with my kids." Time-management experts repeatedly state that tasks also tend to fill up—and sometimes overflow—the slots you allot for them. Being done early with a meeting or a task is a rare occurrence. Generally one meeting has to be ended because there is another you must get to.

Thus dads need to be planners, and they need to learn to prioritize their "meetings." It is the courageous father who says, "I am sorry, I need to cut this call short—I have another appointment," when that other appointment is a daughter's gymnastics meet or a son's piano recital. Or what if that other appointment is the hour you go to the gym? Too many dads miss grandchildren's weddings these days because they never took the time to stay in shape. Heart disease grabs them too early. Dads need to find the proper balance between the worlds they live in: spiritual, mental, social, physical, financial, and family.

So, like the old time-management parable goes: keep these things balanced by putting the big rocks—the most important things—in first. Prioritize the activities on your schedule and block out time for the most important ones first, and then arrange the others accordingly.

worth thinking about

▶ **Hagar thought** she was alone when Sarai cast her and her baby out into the desert, yet God knew right where she was and took care of her.

▶ **The Book of Job** says that God knows everything there is to know about the birds and animals—where they sleep, where they live, what they eat, and how they navigate their migration routes.

▶ **The Book of Genesis** says God knows every language on the planet.

> *Take comfort, and recollect however little you and I may know, God knows; He knows Himself and you and me and all things; and His mercy is over all His works.*
>
> Charles Kingsley

9

question

Do you value what your kids should value?

Are your values intentional or accidental? Taking a simple wallet and calendar test can tell you a lot. As the Bible says, your heart will follow whatever you treasure. In other words, what you spend your money on is what you value; what you spend your time doing is what you treasure. What would these tests show your kids about how much you value them and their futures?

answer

Take two weeks to track what you spend your time and money on. Keep a sheet of paper with you and write down everything you spend and then everything you do every fifteen to thirty minutes of your waking hours. Total them and divide by two. If you discover that you spend more time watching TV than praying, what does that tell you? What if you spend more money on greens fees than you put away for your kids' college educations? This can be a painfully revealing test.

Priorities should start in your heart and be reflected in your words and actions. Too many let their values be steered by the currents in the world around them. More often than not, people today are being influenced instead of being influencers. For dads, it should be just the opposite—dads pass on *their* values to their children and run against the current of cultural moral complacency.

However, before you can influence others, you need to set and follow standards for yourself. You need to ground yourself in your values so that you can pass them on. This comes from your deciding where your time will go and where your money will flow. It starts with your doing what you think is right even when no one else is looking. This will give you the foundation you need for passing on your values to your kids, and it will give them the confidence to stand up for those values among their peers.

worth thinking about

▶ **Integrity starts** by simply letting your yes be yes and your no be no. That means keeping your word, simply always doing what you say.

▶ **In our society** today, standing up for your convictions can be tough—what are you doing to "exercise" your moral resolve? What gives you the strength to always do the right thing?

▶ **Again, your church** is a good place to find a group of men to support you and discuss how to guard your integrity no matter what.

> *It is not what we eat but what we digest that makes us strong; not what we gain but what we save that makes us rich; not what we read but what we remember that makes us learned; not what we preach but what we practice that makes us Christian.*
>
> Francis Bacon

10

question

What is most important about being a dad?

After these first ten questions, your head may be spinning. Yes, there is a lot to being a great dad, but it is not an impossible task. It is certainly about roles—provider, protector, encourager, and so forth—and being an example your kids can respect. If you could boil all of the qualities of a great dad down to one, what would it be? If there is one area that you should really work on, what is it?

answer

It should be no mystery that the most important thing about being a dad is loving your kids. The idea of love has truly been through the cultural wringer to the point it can mean almost anything these days. When looking for a standard for such an important topic, it serves everyone well to return to the source. What did Jesus say about love?

Jesus basically broke love down into four commandments. The first is to love God with all of your heart, mind, soul, and strength. Are you getting closer to God every day with every part of your being? The second and third are to love others as you love yourself. Have you learned to love yourself? And is that acceptance and grace reflected in how you treat others? The fourth is lesser known: Love others the way Jesus has loved you. This is the toughest standard of all—can you love your family just as Jesus showed love to His disciples in the Gospels?

Love is not a feeling; it is how a person relates to others. Jesus' love was preemptive—He loved first and always, whether that love was returned or not. He saw ahead and provided for the future. He prayed events through before they happened. He was also teaching, helping, and nurturing His disciples—and ultimately He was willing to sacrifice His own desires for the good of others. At its foundation, being a great dad is a reflection of that kind of love.

worth thinking about

▶ **Pray for your kids,** and also listen to what God has to say about them. What are His hopes and dreams for their futures?

▶ **Learn to love yourself.** Don't pass your insecurities on to your children. Overcome those fears by learning to look at yourself as God does in the Bible.

▶ **What have you done** to show that you love God today?

> *Love is always supportive, loyal, hopeful, and trusting. Love never fails!*
>
> 1 Corinthians 13:7–8, CEV

question

How do you model keeping God first?

There is no question that more demands are placed on a father's time than in any previous era. Modern conveniences only mean that dads are expected to do more, not that they have more time. Too often fathers are up and out of the house before their children are awake, or they arrive home after the children are already asleep. In such a world, how does a dad model that his relationship with God is the most important thing in his life?

answer

Your kids won't know how important God is to you unless they know how important they are to you. This may seem odd, but if God is just one more thing that takes you away from them, then your dedication to Him will soon seem like one more thing that steals you from them rather than as a blessing on your household. Kids need to see your love for God reflected in your love for them.

They also need to see you living each day trusting in God's strength and wisdom more than your own. When you make a decision that they see, do they see the wisdom of God, or do they see something more arbitrary as the principle behind that decision? Do they hear the same rote prayer every time you pray over a meal, or sense a new part of a continuing conversation that started with your morning quiet time? Do they see your love and reverence for Him in how you walk through each day?

You have to realize that the time you spend with God is not necessarily to model to your kids that they should have daily quiet times, too—though that may be a by-product—but that you sincerely plug into God's strength and direction to order your life each day. It is not simply a habit, but it is where you go to get in touch with God, filled with His wisdom, and empowered to be a great dad. When your kids see God's love for them in your eyes, only then will they know the value of putting God first in everything.

worth thinking about

▶ **In the order** of things you do today, put God first.

▶ **If Jesus is your Lord**, your allegiance to God is greater than any other obligation you have. Your relationship with Him should permeate every one of your daily activities.

▶ **Ministry work isn't** relating to God any more so than cleaning the kitchen is relating to your wife. How do you keep things personal with God?

> *Seek the Kingdom of God above all else,*
> *and live righteously, and he will give*
> *you everything you need.*
> Matthew 6:33, NLT

question

Do your kids have
time with God?

How do your kids relate to God on a daily basis? Do they have a quiet time when you do? Do they pray before they go to bed at night? Do they read the Bible—or do you read the Bible to them—every day? Beyond such duties, how does God direct their daily lives? As they are faced with ethical and social demands at school and with friends, do the scriptures they memorize help them make the right decisions?

answer

Christianity does not work very well only as a religion. Religion tends to be a series of rituals and practices that a person habitually repeats. Religion disciplines a person's habits and practices as he works to be holy and right with God. While religion aids in the pursuit of God, you make a huge mistake if you let it replace that pursuit. Thus, the practices of Christianity have the most meaning if they emerge from your relationship with Jesus rather than being merely a philosophy for living.

When God gave the Ten Commandments to the people of Israel, He added the caveat that those commandments would do little good if the people did not first love God with all their hearts, minds, and strength. Your love for

God is to be reflected in what you talk about with your children when you are sitting with them, walking down the street, or working together in the garage. In other words, loving God is to be an ongoing conversation that overflows into every other area of life.

Your children's time with God starts within this ongoing conversation. It is certainly reflected in going to church, taking Communion together, praying at bedtime, and saying grace before meals, but it should continue in the conversation on the drive home from church, what you thought about while taking Communion, and what is said during meals together.

worth thinking about

▶ Share your testimony of how you come to Jesus with your kids. Tell them about times your prayers were answered in ways you never expected.

▶ Pick one night a week to read a passage of scripture before a meal, and then during that meal discuss how to apply it to your lives.

▶ How do you love God outside of going to church and weeknight fellowships? Discuss how you love God with your family on a regular basis.

> Write these commandments that I've given you today on your hearts. Get them inside of you and then get them inside your children. Talk about them wherever you are, sitting at home or walking in the street; talk about them from the time you get up in the morning to when you fall into bed at night.
>
> Deuteronomy 6:6–7, The Message

question
▼
Do your kids know you love your wife?

Kids need to see love in order to understand it. For them to be able to differentiate real love from what they hear and see about love in the world around them, they need to be able to have a living example of that love constantly before their eyes. The quality of interaction within your family will rub off on the quality of interaction your children have in their social situations. How do you model a selfless, healthy love for your wife before your children?

answer
▼

The fact that God created marriage gives one pause to think. It is easy to gloss over the difficulties of marriage in a book like this, but to be a great dad, you will have to love your wife. Your kids look to how their parents interact in order to define the stability of their world.

While much of the discussion of love today is about the act of "falling into" it, the truth of the matter is that real love doesn't start until the euphoria of attraction wears off. Acting loving only when you feel like it isn't being loving—it is letting your emotions rule and not your will.

How do you treat your wife when you are angry with her? How do you speak to her? How do you relate with her when you are grumpy and tired? Or when you are irritable or frustrated? How about when you are just simply bored? Or how about when she is angry with you? This is where the rubber meets the road with God's love in the family. Loving God's way is a choice, not a fit of emotion. Find a way to diffuse your anger and be civil and polite even when you don't feel like it, and then talk later when you can focus on the issue and not on how angry you were.

worth thinking about

▶ Research is discovering that the very fabric of our culture is held together by the family, and that the family is held together by the strength of the parents' relationship.

▶ Where do you get strength to love your wife when it is the last thing on earth you feel like doing? Take a fresh look at 1 Corinthians 13.

▶ Don't let your feelings always dictate your actions. Decide what your actions will be, and tell your feelings to get in line.

> *The most important thing a father can do for his children is to love their mother.*
> Theodore M. Hesburgh

14

question

Are you still courting your wife?

When you first saw your wife, or discovered you were developing a romantic attraction to her, nothing she did or said bothered you. You set out to win her heart with more enthusiasm than winning a high school sports title, and that enthusiasm came quite naturally. You were creative, came up with great ways to get to know each other, and spared no expense or energy in letting her know you were interested. Has that changed now that you are married?

answer

For most men, the answer to that last question is yes. Being married too soon becomes routine in the rush of responsibilities that husbands face. Becoming fathers only increases that weight of responsibilities. Courting your wife becomes an increasingly lower priority while the time and opportunities for it decrease as well. New parents today tend to trust their children to babysitters less than they did a generation ago, taking away even more opportunities for parents to go out alone together. It doesn't take long beyond that for the children to become almost the sole topic of conversation between husband and wife. This can go on to the point that after the last child is off to college, husbands and wives look at each other and realize they don't even know each other anymore.

Fathers, it is within your power to keep this from happening, and by doing so, increase your stock as a great dad. Your kids should have tons of stories to tell their dates and future children about the crazy things their dad did continuing the pursuit of their mom's heart. You are limited only by your own lack of imagination! And if you can't think of something new, just repeat something you did when you were dating—your wife will be surprised you remembered!

Never stop being the man your wife first fell in love with. Keep pursuing your wife's heart and show your kids how to love. It will become the stuff of legends for your grandchildren!

worth thinking about

▶ What are some of the things you did to win your wife's heart when you were dating? Pull one of them out and see what effect it has on her now.

▶ What are your wife's interests? Get a babysitter and surprise her with a night out pursuing one of her hobbies.

▶ Do you still hold hands and snuggle on the couch? When was the last time you got her a card, flowers, or a little present when it wasn't a holiday?

> *Husbands, go all out in your love for your wives, exactly as Christ did for the church—a love marked by giving, not getting.*
> Ephesians 5:25, THE MESSAGE

15

question

Do you have a regular date night?

Do you take regular time to go out alone with your wife and do something fun together? Are you creative in coming up with things to do? When you go out, is it always something you want to do, or something new you think she will like? Isn't curling up on the couch to watch a DVD with a bowl of popcorn and the kids in bed enough? Why do you have to continue going out after you are married?

answer

One big problem for husbands today is that they never really learned to date. Today, dating seems to be about anything other than what it was intended to be—getting to know a person of the opposite sex better and building emotional and social compatibility with that person. It is about creating one of those special times when you can really talk to another person without anything else in the way to distract you—and it is about having fun together. Your wife also needs a time to shine. You need to let her get dressed up, take her out, and show her off.

As a couple grows in marriage, they change. When they have kids, they change even more. If a couple doesn't continue to date, they don't make time for those heart-to-heart conversations they had when they were first getting to know each other—and soon they begin to feel like strangers. The bond between them becomes weaker, and when it is tested, sparks fly that weren't there in the years before.

Don't fall into the trap of thinking it is a date when there is no time in it for you to interact. Going to a movie or doing some activity like playing miniature golf together is great, but if that is the entire date, then you have missed the point. Set some ground rules—don't get lost in talking about the kids or your work all of the time. This is a time to connect and keep your relationship vital and energized.

worth thinking about

▶ **Check with your** church youth group to start forming a list of reliable babysitters you can call as needed.

▶ **More and more,** young mothers are reluctant to leave their children with a babysitter for the first few years. This can take its toll. If having teenagers babysit your kids makes your wife nervous, find another young couple you can babysit for and trade off with them for nights out.

▶ **Make a conscious effort** to be on the lookout for fun dating opportunities. It is best not to surprise your wife with a date, but you can surprise her with where you are going on your date.

> *A man's greatest treasure is his wife—she is a gift from the LORD.*
> Proverbs 18:22, CEV

question

Is it okay to push your kids in a sport?

answer

Don't force your kids into sports. I never was. To this day, my dad has never asked me to go play golf. I ask him. It's the child's desire to play that matters, not the parent's desire to have the child play. Fun. Keep it fun.

Tiger Woods

question

16

Do you love your family on purpose?

Oftentimes fathers get caught up in the roles they have as breadwinners and protectors of their family and think they have the bases covered if they are providing their family with a comfortable lifestyle and living in a relatively safe suburb. But families need more than that. Kids need to be able to connect with their fathers on a personal level as well. What do you do out of the ordinary to let them know you love them?

answer

Fathers are the foundation of their children's confidence. As such, your support and belief in them needs to be constant and obvious. What son doesn't turn to see if his dad is watching before he steps into the batter's box? What daughter doesn't peek behind the curtain to see if her father is there before a dance recital? To kids, your dependable presence is more important than their ability to get the latest designer fashions.

Kids know they matter to the universe because they know they matter to their fathers. In times of pressure or self-doubt, it will often be your words of encouragement or criticism that come to their minds. Will those words bolster them or undermine their resolve? Will their attitude be one of "can do" or "I quit"? Will they have an inflated opinion of themselves or the quiet resolve to do their best and know they are winners in the long run whether this time is a "success" or not?

Also, what mementos do your kids have of your love for them? Pictures and souvenirs of special family times or vacations are reminders that you were willing to set other things aside and make your kids the center of your world. Surprising them with times to be with Dad— whether you pick them up at school for lunch or sweep them away to do something fun together on a Saturday morning after washing the cars—makes an indelible impression on your kids. Make sure the impression always carries the mark of your love.

worth thinking about

- ▶ **Make a plan** to surprise one of your kids with some Dad time in the next week or two.

- ▶ **What do you find** yourself always saying to your kids? When your kids one day talk with their kids and say, "Well, your grandfather used to always say . . . ," what will they be sharing of your wisdom?

- ▶ **Don't let your work** encroach on your home life too often. Make a point of spending time with your family every evening even if it means putting work off until they are in bed.

> ▼
> *Children learn to smile from their parents.*
> Shinichi Suzuki

17

question

Do you have regular public displays of affection?

For one reason or another, many men are uncomfortable with hugs and kisses in public. This often happens because their fathers were not big on showing affection, so they grew up with a similar inhibition. However, kids need physical contact to grow up with healthy self-images. Babies need to be held, children need to be patted on the back, teenagers need to be wrestled and snuggled with on the couch. Have you hugged your kid today?

answer

Researchers have discovered that babies in orphanages grow up much healthier and stronger if they are regularly held. In fact, many do not survive into their teen years if they are not held at least an hour a day! God has built into every child the need to bond with his or her parents through physical touch.

Sometimes fathers forget this as their children grow older, and especially as daughters reach puberty and start turning into young women. Men can get a little nervous about cuddling with their daughters as much as they did when they were younger, but they shouldn't. These girls still need that physical contact, and if they don't get it appropriately from their fathers, then too often they will look for it among the boys their own age.

As boys reach adolescence, they often express their needs for physical contact by testing their dads' strength with bear hugs and other such tussles. Your attitude should still be "Bring it on!" even though you won't win as easily as you did when they were five. Let your boys learn how to use their strength without hurting others—particularly you!—but don't let them go without a good hug of congratulations once in a while, either.

Do you also kiss your wife and snuggle with her in front of your kids? Appropriate displays of affection for their mother also help your kids establish boundaries for what is and is not appropriate physical contact with the opposite sex. And it doesn't hurt to let your wife know that you are not skittish about letting others know that you love her!

worth thinking about

▶ **Boys will often** reach an age where they act like your hugs embarrass them. Let them have some space, but don't be surprised when they grab you from behind and squeeze—they are just letting you know they are not adults yet!

▶ **Don't ever underestimate** the power of kissing your wife good-bye in the morning and hugging her when you get home—even if it is just to remind her that you love her.

▶ **Do you give** your daughter a kiss good-bye on the cheek when she leaves the house for the day? Do you tell her at least once a day that you love her?

> *He [Jesus] took the children in his arms, put his hands on them and blessed them.*
> Mark 10:16, NIV

question

Should children see their parents fight?

Tensions in the home are tough on kids and seem to be taking a toll on marriages across America. Fierce, emotional battles between parents are too often strong childhood memories, especially for children of divorced parents. While it used to be an adage that parents shouldn't fight in front of their children, more modern thoughts seem to be that such principles are too protective and not honest. Should your kids ever see you fight with your spouse?

answer

Few arguments between spouses are fueled solely by the issue being debated—husbands and wives too often carry stress from their environments, unhealthy patterns carried over from how they were raised, and the hurt of slights they feel from others, whether they were intentional or not. When an issue is contended, all of these things rise to the surface, and disagreements too soon turn into an effort to infuriate rather than solve the matter at hand. Over time, these differences can seem irreconcilable, and homes become battlegrounds rather than sanctuaries away from the chaos of the world.

Too many parents today do not have the self-control to stop an argument before it becomes heated, let alone put it off until a better time. They make the error of either dealing with it when they are too angry or burying it until it builds to an explosive force. The Bible encourages neither, saying it is okay to be angry but not to let it lead to making rash decisions or doing something you will later regret. When you are angry, don't let it prompt you to make emotional attacks; yet also don't let the reason for your anger go unresolved past bedtime.

Your children will inevitably see you disagree with your spouse, but you should have the self-control to be able to either handle that argument civilly or agree with your spouse to deal with it later when emotions are less hostile. This takes quality communication and commitment between parents, and it models proper conflict resolution skills to your kids.

worth thinking about

▶ **Talk with your wife** about how you want to handle disagreements in front of your children. Learn your patterns for disagreements, and create habits to resolve them more productively.

▶ **The Bible says** you should forgive others just as God forgives you. Do you forgive or hold grudges? Walk in forgiveness.

▶ **Your home should** be a place of peace and refreshment, not conflict. Resolve with your wife that the cares of running your household will not so overwhelm you that it affects your kids.

> *A gentle response defuses anger, but a sharp tongue kindles a temper-fire.*
> Proverbs 15:1, THE MESSAGE

19 question

What does it mean to be the family provider?

It is easy for fathers to get lost in their work, justifying that their primary responsibility in life is to provide for their families. But is provision only for material needs? The literature and movies of today are filled with stories of "poor little rich kids" who have everything they could ever ask for, except time with their fathers. Are you providing for your children in all the realms of life: spiritual, emotional, mental, social, physical, financial, and family time?

answer

Working hard and climbing the corporate ladder seems to come naturally to most men. Too often, however, the world of the office becomes all-consuming. Relationships with colleagues at work tend to be easier and more rewarding; praise from bosses and managers can be addicting as you work to put in more hours than you did the last time to get the next promotion. Too many people think, *I just need to do this for now. Then when I get the next promotion, we will finally have enough money, and I can spend more time with the kids.* But that time never comes.

Too many people think that providing for their family is always about earning more money. While earning more money does help, money cannot raise your kids. It can't teach them to develop character and stick to their principles as they grow up. Such things rub off on kids as they spend time with fathers who balance the need to financially provide for their families with the need to nurture and establish them as contributors to their world, secure in the fact that their fathers love them more than anything else except God and Mom.

Financial stability actually has more to do with what you save than with what you earn. Once you have a plan for saving for the future, earning money should be balanced with spending time with your children and rubbing off on them. Your kids would never trade away their time with you for more money, so why would you do that to them?

worth thinking about

▶ **Researchers have found** those who put off immediate gratification for greater rewards later on are more likely to succeed in life. This has a direct application to saving money.

▶ **Take some time** with your spouse and talk about your spending and saving habits. Normally spouses tend to be very different in how they deal with money. Understanding where the other is coming from can make managing money easier.

▶ **Find simple ways** to pass along how you manage money to your kids.

> *He who is taught to live upon little owes more to his father's wisdom than he who has a great deal left him does to his father's care.*
>
> William Penn

question

What is the first step toward financial stability?

How money is dealt with in a family can make a great difference in the peace of your home as well as the quality of your life. If you don't learn to master money, you will serve it all the days of your life, whether you have a lot or only a little. If you want to learn to master money, where do you start? How much money is enough?

answer

The first step toward financial stability is to direct your money rather than allowing money, or the lack of it, to direct your life. Budgeting could be a big part of that, but there is more to mastering money than just having a plan. It also includes your attitude toward money. Is money a tool for you, or is it an end in itself? Will you be insecure about money no matter how much you have in the bank, or does money burn a hole in your pocket so you rarely save anything? Can you give it away freely to help others? If your happiness and satisfaction in life come from money and material possessions, you will have problems no matter how wealthy or poor you become.

Jesus said that it was impossible to have two masters: you can't serve God and money at the same time. But He also said that all the things you need to live are found in doing what is right, seeking Him, and being a blessing to other people. What comes first in your priorities: God or working to earn money? What is first in your spending: giving and tithing or paying bills? Does your contentment come in life from your relationship with God, or from the amount of money you have (or don't have) in the bank?

Come up with a plan for your finances that puts God first, and rely on Him to make it work. It may be tight for a couple of months, but the long-term rewards will be rich in His blessings.

worth thinking about

- ▶ **After you get a paycheck,** what is the first payment you make? Do you give to God first, or do you pay all your bills and just give Him whatever is left over?

- ▶ **The next time** you write a check to your church or a charity, take a moment to pray that the money will be a blessing to the organization.

- ▶ **The average item** bought on a credit card in the U.S. costs more than twice its retail value because most people only make minimum payments. Save and pay cash for large items rather than buying them on credit.

> *Godliness with contentment is great gain.*
> 1 Timothy 6:6, NKJV

21

▼

What should you
be saving for?

Many fathers feel that they can't put away money for the future because they don't make enough. However, families suffer financially because they spend their money first and then save whatever little is left over. Financial experts advise just the opposite: save for the future first, and then enjoy spending what is left. But what should you be putting money away for? Where should you be directing funds before you even buy your groceries or pay your rent?

answer

▼

Financial advisers always say you should pay yourself first, meaning that you should always invest in your future before spending money on something you want today. In other words, direct your money to the things that are farthest in the future before anything else, and then work your way backward in time. This would mean first building up your treasures in heaven, investing in eternal things by giving money to your church and other worthy organizations before anything else. As you give, you will change your mentality about money. It will become a tool in your hand to accomplish what you need rather than be merely a means of getting what you want.

Next, you should be saving for your future and your children's. If you are in your twenties, the dollars you save now will multiply much faster than those you save in future decades. Deposit regularly to your retirement fund and your children's college funds. Get with a financial planner to help you. Get with a lawyer to set up a will and estate plan. You should put money into an emergency fund and let it grow until it reaches two to six times what your monthly expenses are. Then you should save monthly for things you pay for quarterly, every six months, or every year, like car and home insurance, Christmas and birthdays, as well as your anniversary weekend.

It may seem that you have too little left over to spend, but as the different accounts grow, money will take up less and less of your thought life.

worth thinking about

▶ **When you borrow,** interest works against you; when you save, it works for you. That can mean a 20 percent to 30 percent difference between putting money in savings for a large-ticket item versus buying it with a credit card.

▶ **Learn to live** off old money. In other words, you should be living off what you put in your savings months ago rather than the check you just deposited.

▶ **Put your credit cards** in a drawer for a month, and live by spending cash and writing checks.

> *The LORD your God is giving you the land, and he will make sure you are successful in everything you do. Your harvests will be so large that your storehouses will be full.*
> Deuteronomy 28:8, CEV

22

question

How many toys are enough?

The world today is based on consumption, and everything is bigger, better, new, and improved every twelve to eighteen months. As they simply sit down to watch Saturday morning cartoons, children are trained through endless commercials to want the latest, greatest toys. But how many toys do your children—or you—really need? Do you have to have the latest, greatest cell phone, MP3 player, or HDTV? Is your status wrapped up in your stuff?

answer

There is a saying that God doesn't care if you have stuff as long as that stuff doesn't have you. The American tradition of keeping up with the Joneses—making sure the car parked in your driveway and the toys in the backyard are as nice as those parked in the driveways and backyards around you—often changes the consumer culture to a debt culture. How much credit card debt do you roll over each month? Should you be buying that new toy or paying down that balance with the extra money you earned this month?

Ordering your finances generally means that you will need to put off buying some things until later, and that self-control—what Daniel Goleman coined as "emotional intelligence"—is a key ingredient to success and stability. There is nothing wrong with having toys as long as you have first put money away for the future. Everything you buy now with money you are borrowing or should be saving is worth two such items down the road.

As a father, you should be building this principle into your children. What do they do with that hundred dollars they receive for their birthday? Do ten of those dollars go to your church and charities? Do they save part of it? Or do they go out the very next weekend and spend it all on the latest retail-priced game or toy they want? Are you teaching them to master their money?

worth thinking about

▶ **Do you shop** used items for deals or always buy new? Bargain hunting is a hobby of many wealthy people. Then put what you save into an investment.

▶ **Do you impulse buy?** Teach your kids to wait at least twenty-four hours before buying something they just saw and think they want. You will be surprised how often they forget it.

▶ **You should never** buy something with a credit card that you do not have money to pay for in an account earning you interest. Pay off your credit cards each month, or put them away.

> *He is a man of sense who does not grieve for what he has not, but rejoices in what he has.*
> Epictetus

question

Are you teaching your kids to be givers?

Jesus said, "You are more blessed when you give than when you receive." Do you practice this with your kids? Is giving and service to others part of your routine? Are you involved in missions or giving to support a child in a foreign orphanage? Do you volunteer locally at a homeless shelter or aid organization? Do you have things that you do with your kids that earn money to give to a cause you have chosen to support together?

answer

Everyone has three areas from which they can give: their time, their talents, or their treasure. While giving money to a worthy cause is a wonderful thing, spending time working with the disabled, volunteering in a soup kitchen, or delivering groceries to needy homes over the holidays can be the stuff of family memories as much as vacationing or playing together.

Yet teaching your children to be charitable and volunteer gives them much more than family memories. It gives your kids the chance to learn the true joy of giving, even more than putting their dollars and coins into the collection plate at church every Sunday. Giving is the first principle of keeping money from mastering you. Also, as is written in the Book of James, true, pure religion cares for widows, orphans, and those in need. Giving of your time, talents, and treasure keeps the consumer mentality in check as well as adding real value to life; it is what Paul called living the life that is truly worth living.

Great dads are always giving to their families, but you need to instill that value of unselfishness into your children. It is a value that will transform communities—especially if you encourage your kids to get their friends involved. Hopefully, it will be a legacy that you can share with your grandchildren as well.

worth thinking about

▶ **Find places** where you can volunteer with your children. Does your church get together to volunteer regularly in your community or help organize food and clothing drives?

▶ **Take a short-term** mission trip with your family.

▶ **As a family**, select a charitable organization to which you will donate monthly (such as one through which you can sponsor a child in need). Read the organization's newsletter together with your family each time it arrives.

> *We make a living by what we get,*
> *but we make a life by what we give.*
> Winston Churchill

question

24

Are you teaching your kids to be spenders or savers?

Financial pressures on young adults are greater today than ever before. College students receive offers for credit cards before they even have jobs. According to a recent study of thirteen thousand college students, more than 50 percent had five thousand dollars or more in credit card debt, and one-third owed more than ten thousand dollars for their credit card purchases. How are you teaching your children to manage money from a young age? Are your kids learning to be savers or spenders?

answer

Many parents overlook teaching their children about financial management because they feel the money they receive is for presents rather than to begin a retirement account. To a certain point this is true, but the toys kids buy rarely hold the kids' interest for more than a few weeks. Some toys never get played with again after the day they are opened. Why teach your children to waste money on frivolous things? You can help them understand principles of saving while the amounts are still manageable and they have no expenses to complicate their budgets.

From the first cash gift your child receives, you should teach them to give 10 percent, save another percentage you agree upon, and then enjoy the rest. If children can learn to be faithful with little, then you know they can gradually be trusted with more. Some parents urge relatives to spend only half of what they planned to spend on presents for their kids and to contribute the difference to a college fund.

Don't miss the opportunity to teach your children sound financial principles while things are still simple. Your children will have a lifetime to thank you later on. Get them used to having money and not needing to spend it. If they do with their first paycheck what you taught them to do with their first birthday check, you can be assured they will have a good financial future ahead of them.

worth thinking about

- ▶ **Instill in your children** that happiness isn't about what you want, but about what you have. Never buy them things just because they are bored or upset.

- ▶ **When they are** in their teens, let them borrow money from you to buy what they want. But if they miss a payment, "repossess" it until they pay up. It is better to have them lose the use of their iPod at thirteen than to get their car repossessed at twenty.

- ▶ **Teach your kids** to be good stewards of their time, talents, and relationships. These are the stuff of true and lasting wealth.

> *A budget is people telling their money what to do instead of wondering where it went.*
>
> John Maxwell

25 question

How should you handle birthdays and Christmas?

Keeping up with the Joneses is as much about the parties you throw your children and the gifts they bring to the other children's parties as it is about anything else these days. But will your child really remember the expensive birthday party at the local arcade more than games in the backyard? Does your Christmas tree really have to be buried in gifts for it to be special?

answer

Blessing kids with gifts on special days is every parent's joy, as is throwing them a spectacular party, but will they appreciate the price tag more than the love and creativity you put into it? Of course not. That doesn't mean you can't be a little extravagant from time to time, either, but if you are maxing out your credit cards, you are not doing anyone a favor.

Save in advance for birthdays and Christmas presents, and stick to your budget. Make sure your spouse is in agreement that these events are not excuses to tap into your emergency fund. Save a regular amount for them each month.

Be creative. The best parties reflect who your child is rather than the latest fad. Plan the party with your child to make it more memorable. Enlist the help of other parents or siblings for younger kids.

Create Christmas traditions that involve being together more than buying lavish gifts. Write poems, make gifts, and set limits on how much people can spend. Pick out a charity to sponsor each year—and never forget the real reason for the season!

worth thinking about

▶ **Kids should have** crazy memories of things their dads did at Christmastime and on birthdays when they were kids. Did your dad do something you remember well? What memories can you make for your kids?

▶ **Consider shopping sales** in the summer for Christmas gifts you know your child has been looking forward to for some time. Watch for sales on those items and avoid the Christmas rush.

▶ **Use cash to buy** your gifts. Credit cards can get overcharged before you even realize it.

> *For centuries men have kept an appointment with Christmas. Christmas means fellowship, feasting, giving and receiving, a time of good cheer, home.*
>
> W. J. Tucker

question

How should your kids see you speak to your wife?

answer

Dad needs to show an incredible amount of respect and humor and friendship toward his mate so the kids understand their parents are sexy, they're fun, they do things together, they're best friends. Kids learn by example. If I respect Mom, they're going to respect Mom.

Tim Allen

26

▼

What will your financial legacy be?

Will money worries pass from your generation to the next? Will your kids worry about how well off you are when you retire? Will you be helping them provide for their kids' college education? Will your children have hang-ups about money that come from how you raised them? Will they be comfortable with money and using it to build the dreams God has put into their hearts?

answer

▼

The Bible says that a good man leaves an inheritance not only to his children, but also to his grandchildren. Too few realize that the financial decisions and attitudes they make today will affect their children and their grandchildren. According to researchers, the average American millionaire is not the extravagantly wealthy person you see on entertainment television. The average millionaire doesn't live in the fanciest neighborhood or in the biggest house; he doesn't drive the most expensive car or dress exclusively in designer clothing. But what he does have is money in the bank. Millionaires have mastered the art of saving and investing—on average about twenty cents of every dollar; then they save another fifteen "just in case." Few people became millionaires overnight. For most of them, it was a gradual process that developed over decades.

In contrast to this, many lottery winners collect their millions only to be bankrupted within a few years. Why? Because the same spending patterns they practiced before they had money continued when they became rich, and they soon blew it all. Truthfully, state lotteries are a poor investment strategy. You are more likely to be bitten by a shark in the state of Colorado than to win a lottery.

Building a financially secure future happens with each paycheck, not when you have an unexpected windfall. Practice godly attitudes toward money. Money can be something that blesses your kids and their kids for generations to come.

worth thinking about

▶ **For most millionaires**, investing in a specific industry is one of their hobbies. They become experts in that sector and invest in the companies who do well.

▶ **Most millionaires** are careful in managing even small amounts of money. They are the types to carefully save their pocket change, and they never pay retail for anything.

▶ **Most millionaires also invest** in their children. They make sure they have a good education and are headed into a solid career.

> *If you are untrustworthy about worldly wealth, who will trust you with the true riches of heaven?*
> Luke 16:11, NLT

question

▼

How do you help your kids face a frightening world?

Today there is a huge difference between feeling safe and being safe. From the threat of terrorism to Amber alerts, parents are inundated with things that make them concerned for their children's futures. How much of this is passed along to your children? From the early caution of "Don't speak to strangers" to the more confined world children live in—because few parents let their kids wander farther than their backyards—do kids see their world as fundamentally safe or something to hide from?

answer

▼

The first step in handling your child's anxiety about the world is honestly facing your own. Is your home environment a peaceful place, or does your general anxiety permeate the atmosphere? Children are affected by the stress of their parents, whether it is about money, world events, or their family's safety. Facing issues head-on as a couple in a way that alleviates stress in your home will reduce the anxiety of your children.

However, a degree of fear in children actually shows healthy development of their awareness of the world around them. It is not uncommon for a baby to cry a little when separated from Mom and Dad and then settle down quickly. A few years later when the child is a toddler, he may suddenly show more anxiety at parting than ever before. His increased awareness of the world makes him more concerned that something might happen to you when you are not with him, while before he was not even aware that you were gone.

Parents also need to face their fears about their children's fears. Many parents add to their children's anxiety by feeding it rather than helping them face it. They never leave their child with a babysitter, or they pull them out of the church nursery at the first hint they are upset, or they continue to check on them because they are concerned even though their children have settled down. Make sure you are confident about whom you leave your children with.

worth thinking about

▶ **In the natural balance** of parenting, dads tend to help their kids stand on their own, while mothers offer more comfort and nurturing. God's plan is that these sides would balance each other. If you feel these are unbalanced, make a plan with your wife to address it.

▶ **If your child's anxiety** seems excessive, don't hesitate to find a professional in your area to ask about it. Your pastor or family physician is a good place to start.

▶ **Be aware of major** life stresses such as moving, the death of a loved one, or another traumatic event. Such extreme situations often call for extra care.

> *A real love for others will chase those worries away.*
> 1 John 4:18, CEV

28

question
▼
How do you deal with your children's fears?

Whether justified or not, our children's fears are real, whether they are about monsters under the bed, nightmares, or the disappearance or death of a child in your community. What about facing bullies at school, or facing rejection by their peers because they want to stick to their standards? How do you help your children develop the courage to face their fears and overcome them? How do you help them stand up for what is right?

answer
▼

Dads are generally the parent upon which kids build their courage to face the world of darkness, monsters, loud noises, getting sucked down the bathtub drain, and big dogs. Since fear is a normal part of growing up, so is the courage to face and overcome that fear. Fear is meant as a warning sign to keep kids safe, so helping them shamelessly sort real dangers from imaginary ones is important. Never shame a child for coming to you with a fear, but encourage it as the first step in dealing with it. Should something happen with a stranger or another adult that is inappropriate, you want your children to know they can come to you without being scorned.

The key with all childhood fears is taking small steps toward helping your children face them. Going cold turkey might work with some children (for example, forcing them to go to sleep with the lights out), but it won't work for all and isn't recommended. There is no shame in easing your child from having the hall light on, to having the door cracked, to a night-light in their room, or even reading to them from the hallway before shutting the light out. You have to know your children and be willing to spend the time they need to handle these fears on their own. The earlier in their lives you deal with them, the easier it will be on you. Be willing to lovingly take the time to calmly teach them bravery in the face of fear, no matter how silly you think those fears are.

worth thinking about

▶ **Nightmares in the middle** of the night can be tough on your sleep, but unless you want your children to crawl into bed with you every time they have one, take them back to their room and stay with them until they fall back to sleep.

▶ **If there are** recurring fears, find a way to deal with them in the light of day through storybooks, pictures, or other positive tools.

▶ **Deal with fears** calmly. Model the bravery that you would like them to show. Some fears will disappear as they get older.

> *Do not fear, for I am with you.*
> Genesis 26:24, NKJV

question

▼

Who takes care of your kids the most?

Starting with you and your wife, your children's world-view is created through the adults around them. The younger your children, the more they need to be around their parents to anchor that world firmly. Research shows that the strength of families in a community has more to do with success in school than any other factor. Who is with your children the most—a parent, a relative, a day-care worker, or a neighbor?

answer

▼

Too many parents accept without counting the cost the cultural norm that both parents have to work outside the house. By the time you figure in day care, travel expenses, and other costs, the difference of having both parents work may simply not be worth it. Also, there are many part-time options for parents who want to be home for their children. The hours from three to six after kids get out of school and before parents normally get home from work are important times to make sure your kids are in proper after-school care programs or home with you or your wife.

If you choose to place your child in a day care, spend time getting recommendations from coworkers, neighbors, or others in your community and make sure you are happy with their programs and teachers. Sexual abuse is a big concern with parents, so talk with your kids about how comfortable they are with everything they do at school, and let them know that any secrets kept from you are "unsafe secrets." You don't have to go into details, but make sure your kids can talk to you about concerns. Don't neglect getting to know their teachers. They can be great role models in reinforcing your values and helping your children grow more responsible.

worth thinking about

- ▶ **If you choose** to send your children to day care, establish a ritual of hello and good-bye for them that they can count on. Sneaking off will often cause them anxiety once they discover you are gone.

- ▶ **Pick your kids** up on time. There is nothing more disheartening than being the last one to get picked up each day.

- ▶ **If one of the parents** is going to watch the children at home during preschool years, make arrangements to have other kids come over and play every once in a while to help them socialize.

> You need to feel confident that your child is being cared for by people you trust, in a safe environment, and in a situation that allows your child to grow and develop to the best of his or her abilities.
>
> Rose Allen

30

question

▼

Where do your children play?

Kids are natural explorers—they need a world whose edges can be tested but also one where those edges are still safe places to wander. While parents seem to be good at child-proofing their homes, often by trial and error as their children go from crawling to toddling, what about neighborhoods and communities? Are your neighbors part of the safety net for your children, or do you live in a world of strangers?

answer

▼

Two generations ago, especially in rural communities, kids could wander entire days, and no one would worry. If little Johnny and Suzy weren't home for dinner, then you knew they were eating with someone else's family and would come wandering into the house around dark. In your parents' generation, kids learned to call from friends' houses but still wandered blocks away from home and into forested areas to create their own adventures. Today it seems kids barely get to play in their yards, and even then, grade-schoolers have cell phones their parents can track by GPS satellite.

While this extra vigilance seems warranted, is your child's sense of adventure and sociability getting smothered in an ever-shrinking world? There no longer seem to be pickup sports in local parks or gaggles of girls window-shopping down Main Street.

What about working to create a world where neighbors know one another and watch out for one another? What about creating neighborhood space where kids can direct themselves, explore, and you can feel confident they are out of harm's way? Your involvement in creating such a community around your children will go a long way in helping other parents as well—it just takes the will to connect with the people around you.

worth thinking about

▶ In an increasingly suburban world, kids need chances to explore nature more than ever. Find clubs and organizations that teach outdoor skills and go camping, or ones that cultivate your child's sense of exploration.

▶ Do you belong to the local zoo or frequent reading time at the library? Communities often have places where you can go to let your children wander and blaze a trail of their own.

▶ If allowed, kids will fall back to easy activities like television or video games. Do you have set times in your days and weekdays when kids have to leave those off?

> *Every child needs a safe place to fall—a place where he or she can explore things without worrying about failure and judgment.*
> Bill Harley

31

▼

How do you protect your children's innocence?

There seems to be a media and cultural assault on innocence today. No matter how hard you try, television and magazine ads are getting racier, movies and news reports are getting more graphic, and foul language is commonplace wherever you go. Children are simply growing up too fast, and the result is more risky behavior by younger and younger kids. How do you protect your children's innocence so that they can develop a healthy intolerance of immorality?

answer

▼

Innocence is a protective shield for children that allows them to grow up at their own pace, develop self-control gradually as they face challenges they can handle before the ones they cannot, and learn to be resistant to temptation in a world prone to exploitation through the basest of human desires. As a result, movies tend to use sex, horror, and violence to stimulate strong emotional responses rather than to build quality story lines. News reports seem to follow the same pattern—whatever is the most sensational gets the most coverage.

Dads, you have to take the initiative in sheltering your children from inappropriate content. To do this, you must first monitor yourself. Do you have strict standards for what you feel you don't need to be watching or listening to? The garbage-in, garbage-out principle works for you first, and then you can set appropriate standards for your children. Many PG-13 films or teen-rated video games are not appropriate for you to be watching, let alone your kids.

Be wary also of what your kids see and hear when spending the night at a friend's house. Make sure you know parents and their standards before you let your children spend the night, and ask what they will be doing that night or what movies they may be watching. Know your kids and how things affect them. When your kids see something accidentally that you think they shouldn't, talk about it with them. The goal should not be solely to shelter your kids, but to teach them to make healthy decisions.

worth thinking about

- ▶ Scary movies can be fun to watch together, but there is a big difference between a movie that bases its scares on surprise versus a horror film.

- ▶ Learn what you need to do to monitor computer usage and Internet access.

- ▶ Make a point of choosing games or other interactive activities to do with your family instead of renting a video. Read to your children as they go to sleep, even if they have a friend over to spend the night.

> To be innocent is to be not guilty; but to be virtuous is to overcome our evil inclinations.
> William Penn

32

Aren't kids basically good at heart?

Children come into the world as innocent babies, but by the time they are two, "terrible" may seem an under-statement! How does a sweet little bundle of joy turn into a tornado of tantrum in the middle of the supermar-ket floor? If children are born pure, where do they pick up their willfulness? Are they catching it from you as the parent? Don't you just need to let kids figure out right and wrong for themselves?

answer

In recent decades, the belief that all human beings are born good and then are corrupted by the culture has been promoted and adopted without much real support. It is hard to look at a newborn baby and believe this is a creature born in sin, as the Bible supports. However, when you realize the nature of that sin, things begin to make more sense.

All human beings are born selfish. Selfishness is a protec-tive trait for infants whose entire world revolves around their basic needs for survival. Their main means of com-munication are crying and cooing. Selfishness is a good thing in its preservation of self, but a bad thing if it is never harnessed to balance personal needs with the needs of others. As a parent, it is not a matter of letting children discover good and bad on their own, but one of guiding them to bridle selfishness in order to be able to choose good. This takes correction, firm limits on acceptable behavior, and discipline.

At its essence, early parenting is about teaching self-control—helping children to curb their individual desires and be in charge of their will rather than letting circumstances or emotions dominate them. Every child is different, and so how you go about that takes as much learning who your child is as it does learning basic parenting techniques, which rarely come in one-size-fits-all.

worth thinking about

▶ Make sure you are on the same page with your wife about how to discipline your child. Talk with other parents about what has worked best for them, and read parenting books together.

▶ A good deal of research is being done today on teaching "emotional intelligence," a trendy buzz phrase meaning "self-control." Watch for this research in your newspaper and bookstores.

▶ How are you modeling self-control to your kids? Keeping your cool in dealing with your kids will go a long way in showing this. Never let your kids think they are too much for you to handle.

> *Surely I was sinful at birth, sinful from the time my mother conceived me.*
> Psalm 51:5, NIV

33

question

Should you spank your children?

The Bible advocates spanking children, and it goes so far as to say that a person who doesn't ever spank his children must despise them because he is setting them up for failure in life. Many parenting experts today, however, say spanking is harmful and encourages children to solve problems with violence. Is spanking an appropriate means of disciplining children? Or is it something that should be avoided at all costs?

answer

Many people who are healthy and thriving today were spanked as children, and you don't have to go far to find unruly children today who are not spanked and are anything but nonviolent. While experts vary widely on the practice itself, those who endorse it don't treat it as an end-all solution for every disciplinary problem. You have to know your children and know what works best with them. For some, the slightest word will be all you need; for others, a spanking won't even get their attention.

In general, spankings are most effective for younger children, usually preschool. Spankings should never be given in anger, and only when they can be specifically linked to the inappropriate action. Spankings should never replace talking with children—they need to understand why they are being disciplined, that you are disciplining them because you love them, and that once the spanking is over, the issue is over and that they will not be reprimanded again for that action unless it is repeated. The correction should also fit the crime. Spanking should not be the only disciplinary method you use.

As kids get older, sometimes they wish you would spank them rather than giving them a more appropriate consequence to their actions. When children break something, doing chores to earn money to pay for the repairs can be more effective than either physical punishment or grounding. Make sure that your aim is always loving discipline and never frustrated retribution. The aim is to help them make better choices in the future.

worth thinking about

▶ **No discipline is effective** if you have to lose your temper before you will act. Your children should never get the idea they are too much for you to handle. Discipline long before the last straw.

▶ **Never spank** a child for an accident or a mistake. Spank only for rebellion or disobedience.

▶ **Don't forget** that it is also effective to reward good behavior! Catch your child doing things right as well.

> We must combine the toughness of the serpent with the softness of the dove, a tough mind with a tender heart.
>
> Martin Luther King Jr.

34

question

Whom do you let into your home?

A home may not be a man's castle anymore, but it is still his protectorate. As the main person responsible for peace in your home, you need to make sure those who enter there are neither predator nor undermining influence. Certainly, this means caregivers for your children, but also your children's friends, whom they talk with over the phone, chat with on the Internet, watch on television, or listen to on their MP3 players. What or whom do you allow into your domain?

answer

As a protector, you are also a gatekeeper. While it is not always possible to control everything your kids are exposed to, you are ultimately responsible for what happens within the four walls of your home. This is your turf, and you decide who is welcome or not. Of course, it is always good to get help from the co-protector in doing that as well!

Make sure you have solid references for your babysitters. More than one teenager has used the excuse of babysitting to hang out with friends their own parents wouldn't let into their homes. Though it may sound strange, as your kids get into upper elementary and middle school, throw your doors open to your kids' friends, and don't be too quick to judge them on wild looks or strange clothing. Under your roof you have a perfect environment to see who your kids are hanging out with.

How many people let questionable characters into their home through television or movies, characters they would never welcome to sit on their couch? Media and entertainment are also your domain. What is on your teenager's MP3 player? What access do they have to the Internet? Be vigilant about who or what your kids are spending time with, especially in your household.

worth thinking about

▶ **Is your computer** located where you can casually look over your children's shoulders to see what sites they are visiting on the Internet? TVs and computers in kids' bedrooms are generally a bad idea.

▶ **Volunteer to chaperone** for your kids' youth group from time to time or for clubs and activities they participate in. Get to know the friends they are making, and be a positive influence on them.

▶ **If you want kids** to hang out at your house, make sure there are fun things to do like shoot pool, play Ping-Pong, or climb or bounce on something in the backyard—and most important, make sure the fridge is well stocked!

Making your home a place where your teen and her friends will enjoy spending time can go a long ways toward staying in the parental driving seat.
Colleen Langenfeld

question

▼

What are your home-field ground rules?

There is a home-field advantage for all sports teams, and the same is true for your home. As your kids grow older, you should want your house to be a place where your children and their friends like to hang out and where other parents know their kids will be safe. With that in mind, how do you create an environment for kids that is fun, but keeps them safe physically and emotionally as well as allows them to grow in responsibility?

answer

▼

It is up to you and your wife to set the ground rules for your home—the more you can do this with your kids, the smoother things will go. Kids take ownership in rules they help create. Young children need only a few simple rules. As kids get older, the list will grow more complex and the items more numerous. Whereas rules like "No hitting or kicking" will last throughout childhood into adolescence, other rules like how high they need to keep their grade point average to be able to hang out with friends on the weekend can be more negotiable.

Your rules don't change when your kids have friends over, either, except perhaps as it pertains to making guests feel welcome. It doesn't matter what a guest's parent lets him watch or listen to at his home; your standards still stick for your house. And if this is a conflict, you may want to think twice about letting your child visit over there. Kids should understand that rules change with territory.

Kids make noise, and if you want kids to feel welcome in your house, there may be some compromises you need to make in that area. The volume of the music they listen to is still your domain, but if they get a bit rambunctious playing games, you may need to roll with it. If things get out of hand, pull your children aside individually and elicit their help in maintaining your house rules.

worth thinking about

- ▶ **Keep your list** of rules as short and simple as possible. God gave the world only Ten Commandments, after all, and Jesus taught how all of those could be summed up in just two.

- ▶ **Make sure** having friends over doesn't always turn into screen time. Your kids should initiate other activities besides watching movies and playing video games.

- ▶ **Avoid closed doors** when friends are over, but also knock or announce your presence when going into a room where they are socializing. Showing such respect makes them feel more welcome and more likely to respect you in return.

> *Without rules, children live in a state of chaos and disorder which typically invites conflict and behavior problems.*
> Mark Strobel

How are other adult relationships important?

You can tell your uncle stuff that you could not tell your dad. That is kind of the role of an uncle. I feel very much like a father sometimes but sometimes I feel like a teammate.

Dusty Baker

36

question

What's your TV schedule?

Television is a big part of culture today. Kids tend to be mesmerized by anything with a viewing screen—TV, video games, computers and the Internet, even cell phones! How much screen time is healthy? Should you let television babysit your kids when you need to get something done? How do you find a balance between TV watching and other activities your family can be doing together?

answer

The American Academy of Pediatrics advises that until the age of two, there is no reason children should be watching TV, and after that age, parents should limit screen time to two or fewer hours a day. With the average child watching four hours of television daily plus video games, it might mean some changes not only in your kids' schedules, but in yours as well! If your children are going to have a healthy relationship with TV, computers, and handheld video games and music players, the first thing you might have to do is change your own habits.

Fill your family room with things to do besides watching TV. Have a shelf with books, crafts, puzzles, and games, and a suitable table at which to do them. When you come home, open a book rather than flick on the TV. Pick out the shows you like, and limit everyone to a preset number of hours a week. Don't turn the set on without already knowing what you are going to watch. If you need to, get a DVR so that you can record your shows, and then you can also fast-forward through the commercials!

Certainly there will be exceptions for the big game or an extended movie night, but don't fall into the trap of letting your television and computer control your time or rob your kids of being able to organize themselves quietly without being mesmerized by a dancing dinosaur or a fast-action cartoon. Welcome TV only on your terms, and then spend the extra time being a fun dad.

worth thinking about

► **Consider the cost benefit** of paying for cable or satellite television each month. For the amount of time you want to actually watch TV, would it be cheaper to rent the shows you like and then invest the savings for a family vacation?

► **Especially if you** have school-age kids, consider not turning the television on at all on school nights (Sunday after 6:00 p.m. through Thursday).

► **Do you have** a way to limit, filter, and regulate Internet use for your family? Do you have the V-chip activated on your TV?

> *The more TV that your children watch, the more problems they will have with attention, in school, with self-control, and with each other.*
> Charles Fay

question

▼

Is your home a creative environment?

If you turned the television off (including the game console), what would your kids do? Is your home a place where your kids can find creative or interactive activities to do if a friend comes over? Are there games accessible? Craft materials? Books to look at and read? Is your yard a place where they can go and play together? When you get an "I'm bored" on a beautiful summer afternoon, where do you direct your children to use their imaginations?

answer

▼

Don't let your family room become a TV room. Have lots of things to do there and places to do them. Do your kids have a creative corner where they can start projects and leave them out? Creativity can be messy, so if you confine it to a table that is not also your coffee table—a place where a puzzle can stay, games can be undisturbed, or a craft can be started and left to be finished later—then the space will still be livable even though everything isn't always put away. Just make sure that space is taken care of before it is left—glue bottles are closed, things aren't scattered all over the floor, and unnecessary debris is cleared.

When you get home from work, go to this area and see what is happening. Comment on crafts being assembled, or start a game or puzzle and then let your kids join in. Get a book and sit down to read, and invite your kids to do the same. Expect things to be a little noisy if your kids are working or playing at the "creative" table while you are trying to watch a game. Enjoy their self-organization. Also organize quiet times in that room with the TV off to encourage reading. Doing this the last half hour before bed can be a great way of getting kids settled for the night. Being in the same room reading or doing different activities can set a great example for when crafts and games have to be traded in for homework.

worth thinking about

▶ Make creative areas appealing by using color and size-appropriate furniture. Use boxes and shelves to keep things organized, even if they are not always neat.

▶ Do you have creative hobbies such as building models or working with remote-control cars or airplanes? If so, is there a creative space for your kids near where you work on these?

▶ As kids get older, clear out the picture books and add chapter books. Add reference books so that this creative area turns easily into a homework area.

> Children, like adults, need time to be alone to think, to muse, to read freely, to daydream, to be creative, to form a self independent of the barrage of mass culture.
>
> Pat Farenga

38

question
▼
Do you inspect what you expect?

Chores are an important way for kids to learn responsibility and feel that they have a part in the success of your home. The same is true for keeping grades up and studying. Do you have set expectations for things your kids need to do around the house? If so, how do you keep track of whether or not they have been done correctly? Do you and your wife make regular inspections?

answer
▼

Making the inspection of chores as objective and regular as possible, especially while your kids are younger, can eliminate a lot of strife in your home. If you want your children to clean up their room, for example, help them clean up their room to an acceptable standard and let them know that every night just before bedtime you will be inspecting. Then take them into their room long enough before bedtime that if there are things to be cleaned, they can be done before you tuck them in for the night.

Having a chart is also great for this—if it is done, give them a sticker; if not, leave it off; if they are close, then let them do a quick cleanup to get things up to snuff. Don't give in to the temptation to get angry if it isn't done or to nag your kids throughout the evening. The more objective you keep it, the better. Give them some kind of privilege status tied to having their chore chart 90 percent full—it could be screen time over the weekend, for example.

Developing a routine for this will help both you and your kids. The toughest thing will be forming the habit of inspecting your kids' chores regularly and not getting emotional if the chores are not done correctly. It will take a few weeks to establish a new system, but the benefits will last a lifetime. Be diligent in teaching your kids to look after their own areas and help keep your household shipshape.

worth thinking about

▶ **Keep chores simple** while your kids are younger. As they get older, they should not only be in charge of their own areas, but keeping shared areas such as the kitchen and living room cleaned up as well.

▶ **Allowances shouldn't** be tied to chores—it should be money they can use while living in your house. If kids need extra money, let them know they can earn more by doing your chores.

▶ **As kids get older,** throw all the chores that need to be done into a hat and let everyone in the household divvy them up and negotiate over who does what.

> *Children with a good self-concept tend to have a lot of friends, do their chores regularly, and don't get into trouble in school—they take responsibility as a matter of course in their daily lives.*
> Jim Fay and Foster Cline

question

▼

How do you settle disputes between kids?

A major factor of peace in your home is keeping your kids at peace with one another. Sibling rivalry can be an ongoing war in your home, and parents can become caught in the cross fire. How do you diffuse it? How do you encourage your kids to get along without your having to intervene every five minutes? How do you get your kids to resolve their own disagreements peacefully?

answer

▼

Too many dads look at misbehavior or disputes between their kids as problems for them to solve. Such things are inevitable. You can step in and dictate a short-term judgment, or you can use the incident as an opportunity to teach your kids how to problem-solve. Parents too easily fall into the mistake of rescuing kids from their problems or decreeing solutions to disputes they are involved in only after the fact. What are you teaching your kids if you are always making their problems your problems and never forcing them to solve them for themselves?

Don't pick up the gauntlet your kids throw down for each other unless someone's safety or the breaking of a house rule is involved (and then, deal with the breaking of the rule, not the cause of it). If your kids create problems with each other, don't take away the opportunity for them to resolve the issue. Teach kids to respect one another's property and space, but also teach them about sharing.

Give them simple tools for deciding something if they disagree, something like doing rock, paper, scissors. When they come to you to settle a dispute, make suggestions and let them go back and apply them. Emphasize responsibility for both of them to resolve the issue, and don't take sides—certainly you will have higher standards for the older sibling, but hold both accountable to respect and love the other. You won't be able to end every dispute, but at least you will be instilling in your kids skills to diffuse conflicts for themselves, and you will be facing fewer in the future.

worth thinking about

- ▶ **Have settling disputes** part of your house rules. Always speak to one another respectfully and model this when you discipline your kids.

- ▶ **Stay as objective** and calm as possible. If the kids are too loud in settling their argument, deal with the noise level as you would any other house rule.

- ▶ **Don't get sucked** into making threats you can't follow through on. If you are not sure at that instant what consequences you want to enforce, let them know you will get back to them on it later.

> *The beginning of strife is like releasing water; therefore stop contention before a quarrel starts.*
> Proverbs 17:14, NKJV

question

Do you have family meetings?

How do you deal with troublesome issues in your kids? Do you deal with each thing as it comes up, or do you let things go until you are so fed up you explode? How do you divide up chores and responsibilities in your home? Do you make a list and assign the chores, let your wife handle them, or let your kids bargain over what needs to be done? Do your kids have a forum where they can be heard objectively by everyone?

answer

As children get older, they should have more stock in making decisions in your home. You may be the CEO who sets the overall framework of how things should be run, but just like a good employer, you want to encourage individual creativity and initiative in the specifics of how things are done. Children, especially teens, need to develop decision-making skills, and making decisions together is a practical way of teaching such skills.

As in any environment where people need to interact with one another, communication of concerns, hurts, and disagreements is necessary to keep bitterness and resentment from developing. Strife, even when below the surface, eats away at everyone in the household, and nothing good comes of it. So if people know that there will be a time to voice their grievances and that they will be heard and dealt with honestly, they are more likely to work things out than continue to simmer until they explode.

However, family meetings can be drudgery as well. It isn't one more opportunity for you to lecture. Don't solicit honest criticism and then not listen to it. Don't tell your kids you are going to let them decide things and then arbitrarily make all the decisions yourself. Use these times to listen and take the pulse of your family's relationships. Encourage siblings to listen to each other and work together rather than against each other. And keep it fun. Family meetings should be one more part of your children's fond family memories, not "Oh, do you remember when Dad used to make us do those meetings?"

worth thinking about

▶ **Keep the meetings** fun and brief; always start and end on time. Use the meetings as the time you distribute allowances. Begin and end each meeting with prayer.

▶ **Do something together** immediately afterward. Following the meeting with a movie or game can keep the communication going.

▶ **Give your kids** responsibilities to report back on at the next meeting. It helps them develop follow-through and confidence in their problem-solving abilities.

> *Courage is what it takes to stand up and speak; courage is also what it takes to sit down and listen.*
> Winston Churchill

41 question

Do you spell love: T-I-M-E?

The tides of men's lives are often very strong, sweeping them off-course so gradually that it takes decades to notice. The world of career can easily overshadow every other aspect of life as a father works to solidify his family's future. Yet children seem to grow up the fastest when you aren't looking. Are you setting aside time to invest in your children now when it matters most? Do you make a conscious effort just to have your kids around you?

answer

Time can be the most slippery element in the universe. If not managed properly, it too easily passes, and fathers quickly find themselves trying to make up for the neglect of a distant past. Unfortunately, you can't leave relationships in the deep freeze while you busily develop another part of your life and then pop your relationships in a microwave later like a frozen burrito. Whether with your wife or with your kids, love means nothing if you don't set time aside every day to communicate and be with them. For dads, this means finding a balance between work, play, and home—and not squandering your waking hours.

God's admonition for raising wise children is that it is to be accomplished while you sit in your house, walk along the way, lie down, and rise up. This speaks of consciously letting your kids be around you and looking for opportunities to teach them in every aspect of life. Certainly dads need some time to themselves, but can you also find ways for your kids to be with you no matter what you are doing? Can they sit at a table and quietly do their homework while you do your work? Can they hand you tools while you fix the lawn mower?

The great thing about this is that it doesn't take a lot of preparation; you simply need to organize yourself to be truly available. You'll be surprised what they—and you—get out of just being together.

worth thinking about

- ▶ **Some dads** put their kids to bed and then go to bed themselves so they can get up and go into work early instead of staying late. Working while your children sleep can give you more time with your family.

- ▶ **Quality time** is still important. Make sure you set the stage for deeper levels of conversation as your children are growing up. Be ready for quality time to happen spontaneously as well.

- ▶ **Sometimes creating** more family time is as easy as turning off the television.

> *Quality is no substitute for quantity when it comes to family time.*
> Gary Smalley

question

How do you speak to your child?

In a world filled with people talking, a father's words to his children leave impressions like no others. There are probably things your father spoke to you that still ring in your ears, even though it has been years since you heard them. Fathers' words can be foundations for a prosperous, healthy future, or they can be tumbling blocks that eat away at confidence and corrode self-worth. How will your children remember the words you've spoken to them?

answer

A father's words to his children operate on several frequencies—there is a surface level, but under that are the faith, love, and confidence behind your words, or the disappointment, condemnation, and aggravation you let slip through. Too often, a father's words carry with them his personal frustrations, and over time these leave all but visible marks on his children's souls. Purpose that every word you speak to your children will edify them and set them on a straighter path for the future.

Even in correction, your words need to be filled with love and confidence in your kids. The Bible says that God disciplines those He loves and that His words are for reproof, correction, and training in righteous living. Another passage states that God's words always build up, encourage, or console. Your words should do the same. This doesn't mean that you should never let your kids see you are angry. It does mean, however, that you should never let your anger determine what you say to your kids. Anger need not be overwhelming.

Your children will build their self-image on your words and actions. Choose your words wisely, and fill your children with confidence that they have a bright future ahead of them, even if they need to make some adjustments first. Communicate the pride you have in them for who they are becoming.

worth thinking about

▶ Don't get dragged into an argument when your child or teen is upset. Both sides should be self-controlled in order to have a profitable discussion. Tell your kid you would be glad to talk about the issue further when you are both calmer.

▶ Sometimes words can seem insincere if you put too much praise into them. From time to time simply let your children know you noticed they did something good without attaching words of approval after the comment.

▶ Lectures are never as effective as concise and specific correction.

> *Words kill, words give life; they're either poison or fruit—you choose.*
> Proverbs 18:21, The Message

question

Do you share interests with your kids?

What do you like to do with your kids beyond playing games or working on crafts in your family room? Beyond going to watch their soccer games or attending their recitals? Do you have hobbies you pursue together? Are there things you like to do you can share with them, or do you share any common interests? Are there also other activities you can pursue with extended family or other fathers and kids at your church?

answer

Great dads plant pieces of themselves in their kids and let them grow. They share their hobbies and interests in a way that is not overwhelming but captures their children's attention. They share them in a way that savors the time spent together more than accomplishing the tasks at hand. Great dads enjoy mistakes for their uniqueness and the opportunities they give for teaching moments.

Whether you are building ships in a bottle or just cleaning the garage, kids like to be with their dads. The key to making the most of your time together is really patience. Kids want to help but are often too young to be of any real assistance, so task-focused dads send them away to get things done faster. But what does it hurt for kids to sweep the same pile of dust around while you do the real work? While you are doing your intricate work on a model, can they do something alongside? It might just be to hold the glue bottle, but let them be there with you. As they get older, they will build the skills to do these things for themselves.

Plug into your kids' interests as well. Let them explore different hobbies to see what they take a liking to. One good thing about having kids in clubs is they learn different skills while doing various activities. You can be there with them and see what they like, then explore those things when you have time together on a free night or over a weekend.

worth thinking about

▶ **Make sure** you are not overbearing in your attempts to share your interests with your kids. Take things slowly. Too many dads burn their kids out on sports, for example, because they push them too hard, and the kids never develop the love of the game for themselves.

▶ **There will be** activities that you share with your kids one-on-one, and others the entire family shares together. Make room for both.

▶ **Are there also** activities you can share across generations? Your parents, your kids, and you? What about with uncles and cousins?

> *It is admirable for a man to take his son fishing, but there is a special place in heaven for the father who takes his daughter shopping.*
>
> John Sinor

question

44

Do you have date nights—with your kids?

In the hustle and bustle of daily lives, homework, your work, and chores, parents too often forget to take regular time out to focus on each of their children and have time with them one-on-one. Individual time is rarely possible at home, but what if you take your son or daughter out? Do you have a regular time each month or every few months to go do something fun with each of your children?

answer

Kids tend to blossom under the individual attention of their dads. They treasure times they have Dad all to themselves and can soak up the attention that lets them know they matter to the universe. It is a time for them to be able to say, "Daddy, watch this!" And nothing in the world can distract you from doing just that.

Though your creativity in such outings is part of the memory making, taking your kids out doesn't have to be extravagant. Pick someplace you can let them cut the path. Museums, zoos, aquariums, concerts, or even just the mall are easy getaways to new experiences for your kids. Then spend the time focused on them. Let them jabber away while you listen. Learn about their likes and dislikes at school, their friends, what they wish they could do, and what they want to become. Let them ply you with questions.

As their kids near their teens, some dads begin a regular day a week to take their son or daughter to breakfast in the morning before school or pick them up for lunch. Set up a question trade—you ask them any one question you want, and they ask you any one question they want. No holds barred. This creates an honest, safe atmosphere to talk about some of the tough issues and find out where your kid stands on them, as well as for you to slowly take some of the mystery out of becoming a responsible adult.

worth thinking about

▶ **Just as with** your wife, make time for some quality talk when you go out with your son and daughter. Make sure all the time isn't taken up with an activity.

▶ **This doesn't always** have to be formal. For younger kids, it could be out to the playground and then off to the ice-cream shop; for adolescents, evening or weekend outings are more fitting.

▶ **Work talking** about God into your discussions. What does your child think God is like? How does your child experience God's love and pass it on to others?

> Teach [My ways] to your children. Talk about them wherever you are, sitting at home or walking in the street; talk about them from the time you get up in the morning until you fall into bed at night.
> Deuteronomy 11:19, THE MESSAGE

question

Are your kids too busy for you?

The minivan and the soccer mom are a staple of most suburban communities these days. Kids who don't have activities three or four nights a week are pretty rare. While you are adjusting your schedule to spend more time with your kids, are your kids' schedules open for time with you? Are they overbooked with dance classes, sports practices, youth group, and other clubs? Do your kids have a couple of nights a week just to be home?

answer

Researchers advocate that kids who participate in three or four hours of activities a week—whether sports, music lessons, or some other activity—are less likely to get involved with risky behaviors such as drug and alcohol abuse, bullying, or premarital sex. Those same advocates also list at least two nights at home a week with nothing special to do as another healthy factor for budding adolescents and teens.

While everyone wants to live in a great neighborhood, parents often miss the temptation that goes along with it—competing with your neighbors to have the best, brightest, and most active kids. The lure is to have your kids in every activity your neighbors' kids are in, and before you know it the only real time you get to spend with your kids is driving them from one activity to another.

You need to structure free time for your kids into their schedule just as diligently as activity time. This is easier for younger children, but by the time they are preteens, they will want to add hanging out with friends to their schedule as well. While teens need to develop their independence, more than a night or two a week hanging out at the mall with nothing specific to do is a recipe for trouble. If you keep your home a welcoming place for kids to hang out, this will encourage more time doing things together as a family as well.

worth thinking about

▶ **Prioritize your children's** schedules just as you would your own. Help them find a balance between their activities, grades, friends, and family time.

▶ **Do your** adolescent children have specific written goals? Take time to help them develop some as well as regularly review them and align their time with them.

▶ **You should have** an amount budgeted for your kids' activities. Work with them to stay within that budget or help them raise money if they want to do things that exceed what you have allotted.

> *Everybody today seems to be in such a terrible rush; anxious for greater developments and greater wishes and so on; so that children have very little time for their parents; parents have very little time for each other; and the home begins the disruption of the peace of the world.*
> Mother Teresa

question

How important is it to stay married?

answer

Studies show that children best flourish when one mom and one dad are there to raise them.

John Boehner

question

Where are your children's "offices"?

Where do your kids do their homework? Do they sit at desks in their rooms, work at the kitchen table, or just grab a spot wherever they settle down? For most homework today, kids need access to a computer. Do you have one in a public place where your kids can work, or do you let them use a notebook computer that floats around the house?

answer

Research has shown that kids generally do better in school the more stable their homework environment is. While desks and working in their rooms on their own may work for older kids—juniors and seniors in high school—it is better if kids have their homework "offices" at a kitchen table or breakfast bar while someone is cooking dinner, cleaning up, or just hanging around. It is also good if this happens with relatively the same schedule each week—something difficult to establish with the many after-school activities and sports that most kids have today.

A computer with Internet access is needed to do most homework now, whether kids are doing research, typing a paper, or reading a textbook on CD. If you take the right precautions, Internet predators or inappropriate content will not be as much of a problem as the Internet will be a distraction from keeping on task. Surfing the Net is more addicting than channel surfing, and kids can sit for hours at the computer researching the latest spring styles at their favorite clothing store. Have a password for your Internet access, and turn it on only when needed. Have your computer in a public place where you can easily glance over a shoulder in passing. The key is to have them working near where your wife or you are, and helping them stay focused for an hour or so each night. Their grades will show the effects of this.

worth thinking about

- ▶ **If you have** an office where you routinely work evenings, set up a homework space in that room as well and work side by side.

- ▶ **A lot of schools** are offering online grade books where you can monitor your children's assignments and progress. Take advantage of these to help them stay caught up.

- ▶ **Try not to** always bring work home so that you can be available to help your kids in the evenings. Though some of the homework may be beyond what you remember, ask questions to help them figure it out for themselves.

If possible, set up a quiet, comfortable study area with good lighting and the school supplies that your children need. This can be almost anyplace in your home; you don't need a special room.

National Education Association

47 question

Are your kids explorers or isolationists?

How do your kids face the world? Are they eager to get out and experience things, or do they view the world as a dangerous place to be avoided? Do they have the spirit of the man who took his one talent and buried it in the ground, or the spirit of those who invested it to multiply what they were given? Is life an adventure for your children or a bit too scary?

answer

The attitudes you adopt toward the world are generally caught by your kids. As you think about the question above, do you think of yourself as an explorer or someone who is trying to keep the losses at a minimum? If you have the latter attitude, how do you turn it around?

Every father wants to pass on a zest for life to his kids yet not deny the realities of its dangers and pitfalls. If you raise your kids to be creative self-starters who avoid the temptations of risky behavior throughout adolescence, and if you ground them well in the values of following Christ, you have started them off right. If you also instill in them a desire to search out and embrace God's purpose and calling for their lives, adventure is unlikely to be a problem—God will keep them stretched and growing!

Encircle your kids with men and women of faith who will mentor them with you in the fruit of the Spirit that build hope and faith for the future. Encourage them in good works. Send them to church camps and on short-term mission trips in the summer to give them a taste of serving God in a different culture or environment. As they grow older, don't keep them completely locked away in a protective bubble so that the first time they experience the world is when they graduate from college. Help them develop the self-control to face the world and maintain their integrity, as well as see that no challenge can go unconquered if God is on their side.

worth thinking about

▶ **Your church youth group** is a great nurturing ground for kids to find the purpose God is calling them to in life. Are your kids plugged in there? Are you plugged in to help there?

▶ **How do your** kids face challenges in school, sports, or other activities?

▶ **What adventures** have you shared with your kids? Take them camping, rafting, or to an evangelistic outreach with your church. Work with them in a soup kitchen, or volunteer to help provide emergency relief after a storm.

> *My father used to play with my brother and me in the yard. Mother would come out and say, "You're tearing up the grass." "We're not raising grass," my dad would reply, "we're raising boys."*
>
> Harmon Killebrew

question

Are you nurturing your children's gifts and talents?

Fathers provide a balance between a safe haven and a gentle push out into the wilderness to blaze a unique trail and experience life unfiltered. As such, fathers are teachers and guides—coaches with trained eyes who see potential and bring it to competence and achievement. What gifts do you see planted in your children? What are you doing to develop these gifts and to refine and train their talents?

answer

The story has been told thousands of times: an old coach sees something in a young athlete that no one else notices—a raw, undisciplined strength that the world has all but beaten down. Taking the young talent aside, he trains him and puts him through hard workouts that the boy would normally have been too lazy to endure except for the attention and driving encouragement of the coach. Then one day, the youth emerges to become a champion. That is the story of *Karate Kid, Rocky, My Fair Lady*, and dozens of other classic stories—all of them essentially stories of orphans who finally find father figures who inspire them to greatness.

Being a great dad is being a coach for life. Sometimes dads walk a fine line between being the disciplinarian and the raving fan. Every coach knows his players sometimes have to be pushed to do their best, while at other times, pulling them aside for a special word of encouragement will instill the confidence to try again.

worth thinking about

▶ **Spend time** talking with your children about their hopes and aspirations. What do they like doing? How can you provide opportunities for them to grow in areas in which they are interested?

▶ **No skill or ability** is mastered without hard work, and kids rarely have what it takes on their own to stick through the tough work needed to become good at something. Be there for them, support them, and encourage them to stay the course.

▶ **Your kids** can't do everything, and their interests will change as they grow up. Be their wise counsel for when it is right to quit something so they can focus more time on something else.

> When we teach a child to draw, we teach him how to see. When we teach a child to play a musical instrument, we teach her how to listen. When we teach a child to dance, we teach him how to move through life with grace. When we teach a child to read and write, we teach her how to think. When we nurture imagination, we create a better world, one child at a time.
>
> Jane Alexander

question

Do you read with your son or daughter?

Leaders are readers. Though video and media are developing at ever-increasing rates, books are still the greatest doorway into the knowledge and wisdom of the ages. There is nothing like a story time for young children to paint a picture in their imaginations. Do you take the time to share with your children the stories you grew up on and loved as a child? Do you read to them every night before they go to sleep?

answer

There is a reason Jesus taught in stories. People tend to remember stories, and their lessons can last a lifetime. Today we are fortunate to have a wealth of stories that teach character and wisdom, from the works of Frances Hodgson Burnett and Laura Ingalls Wilder to C. S. Lewis and John Bunyan, just to name a few. Books are gateways into rich worlds to be explored with your kids.

Making a habit of reading with your children from a young age is a wonderful way to be with them as well as to pull them away from the television set. The stories you read will become part of the fabric and shared culture of your family, the settings of the games they play with each other, and the seeds of the adventures they will write themselves. After a long day at work, sitting down to read with your kids for twenty to thirty minutes can often seem taxing, and it may be the last thing in the world you want to do, but don't miss the opportunity. Your children are small for only so long, and you will treasure each moment you spent reading to them while you could still fit them in your lap.

Fathers and mothers who read to their children introduce them to the world of literature. Curl up with your kids and one of your favorite books tonight. It will be the beginning of a lifetime of adventures to share.

worth thinking about

▶ **Take time** to read the Scriptures with your children. Read to them from the Gospels, the Psalms, and the Bible stories you have always treasured.

▶ **Research shows** that children who grow up being read to from the time they are born make better readers later in life. It plays a bigger factor than any other technique or curriculum that is used to teach reading.

▶ **When you are done**, don't just close the book, kiss your children good night, and turn out the lights. Talk with them about what you just read. It is the first step in developing their speaking and thinking skills.

> *Children are made readers on the laps of their parents.*
> Emilie Buchwald

50

Do your children know you believe in them?

Every child is hungry for his or her father's approval. While many fathers love their children deeply, they don't always communicate that love in a way that kids know their dads are pulling for them and that their dads believe in their abilities. Is your confidence in your son or daughter firmly set in their minds as they meet each new challenge? Do they have the confidence to face new things because they know you think they can?

answer

There is sometimes a fine line between being supportive and being phony. Kids take empty praise in one of two ways—either it feeds a warped sense of who they are or it causes distrust of the person offering the flattery. Educational models out of the 1960s and 1970s proposed that teachers praise kids for everything they did to bolster their self-esteem. The result seemed to be more kids who didn't know right from wrong and more kids with an attitude of entitlement that outweighed any actual merit.

True self-esteem comes from constant loving support from both parents. It comes from consistently matching consequences to actions and catching kids doing something good and noticing it. It comes from being there for their plays, games, and recitals. It comes from helping them with their homework and coaching their activities as best you can. It comes from encouraging them when they are disappointed, holding them accountable to do their best, and letting them know they have what it takes to do even better in the future.

Your confidence in them will undergird them when they know you think they are capable of solving things for themselves and yet are also there to help.

worth thinking about

▶ **Be careful** about taking your kids' side too quickly against teachers or coaches. Don't undermine the authority of other adults in their lives.

▶ **Always take** a long-range view with your child's failures. Failures are easily turned into successes with a little diligence and training. Pushing kids hard when they are too young will often make them burn out rather than build toward success.

▶ **Working on skills** is just one more opportunity for you to spend quality time with your kids.

> *By profession I am a soldier and take pride in that fact. But I am prouder—infinitely prouder—to be a father. A soldier destroys in order to build; the father only builds, never destroys. The one has the potentiality of death; the other embodies creation and life. And while the hordes of death are mighty, the battalions of life are mightier still.*
>
> Douglas MacArthur

question

Should you be your children's best friend?

Many parents today seem to want to be buddies with their kids, but is that the relationship you should have in order to be a great dad? What does it do to your relationships with your sons or daughters if you try to win their affection by doing or buying things for them all of the time? Is this really being a friend to them?

answer

Friends will come and go as your children grow up, but you won't. There will be times that you hang out together and do things that friends would, but at other times you will have to call them on the carpet to be responsible for their actions. Nothing can get in the way of your holding your kids accountable and helping them grow toward healthy self-directedness and trustworthiness. If being their friend compromises your role in helping them grow in responsibility, then you are as bad as peers who lead them in the wrong moral direction.

A great dad has many of the characteristics of a great friend. Your kids can always depend upon you to do what is right and to encourage them to do the same. They can rely on your sticking to your word. They can share things with you in confidence and always go to you in a time of need. You will always be there for them, even when all others have abandoned them.

None of this, of course, is based on their liking you all of the time. Dads have to make some tough calls, and sometimes their household approval rating plummets. While friends are swayed by trying to fit in or making poor decisions, great dads stay the course of holding to what is best for their kids, whether they agree with it or not. If such tough love is consistent and logical, eventually your kids will know for themselves what is right and that you never stopped being on their side.

worth thinking about

▶ Friendship generally starts with common interests, time spent together, and open communications. You should make room for these each day with your children.

▶ A big part of friendship is being open and honest with one another. When Jesus called the disciples His friends, it was because He was open with them about His Father's plans and promises for the earth.

▶ Proverbs says that friends sharpen friends. Is your relationship with your kids sharpening them or indulging the wrong impulses?

> This is the very best way to love. Put your life on the line for your friends. You are my friends when you do the things I command you.
>
> John 15:13–14, The Message

52

question

Is attending church important?

There seem to be fewer and fewer slots for parents to spend time with their children these days. Many kids have activities almost every night of the week, and weekend time is filled with sports, activities, birthday parties, and finally getting some time to catch up on their homework. Churches generally have services Sunday morning, Sunday evening, and Wednesday night, so how important is it to be there every time the doors are open?

answer

Priorities seem to take a lot of negotiating these days. The order never really changes, but each area must find trade-offs with others in your weekly schedule, and attending church is no exception. The question then becomes what your purpose is in going to church. Is it a duty or an integral part of your family's culture?

Your kids will catch your values primarily by what they see you spend your time on. They know you love them because you spend time with them. They know work is important to you because you get up every day and leave the house as they are getting ready for school. And they will know that church is important to you in the same way. The more consistent you are in attending, the more crucial they will see it as being. Of course, they will still want to rebel against it as they grow older. This is both a test of your resolve and a normal part of kids' testing their own convictions.

If you attend church every time the door is open but never pray with your family at home or talk with them about what it means to be a Christian, it is just one more activity that is taking you away from interacting with your children. Spending Wednesday or Sunday night at home being with your kids instead of attending services isn't a bad thing if you are also "living church" every day. Going to church should be an outgrowth of your faith, not a replacement of it.

worth thinking about

▶ **If you are** on vacation with your family—especially if you are camping—have a church service of your own. Have each member share a song or a favorite scripture and pray together.

▶ **Don't let Sunday** mornings be rushed. Use getting up for church as an excuse to have breakfast together before heading out the door. Don't turn the TV on.

▶ **Pray for your pastor**, Sunday school teachers, and church every once in a while when you pray at bedtime or over your meals.

> *Let us consider one another in order to stir up love and good works, not forsaking the assembling of ourselves together . . . but exhorting one another.*
> Hebrews 10:24–25, NKJV

53

Does your community value kids?

Active children's and youth programs are an essential part of any neighborhood, city, or growing church. Does your community seek out and engage its youth, or are the youth mostly an afterthought in planning events, programs, and goals for the future? Where can you fit into bolstering such programs? Who are the key people creating youth programs in your community? Do they share your values or have conflicting personal or political agendas?

answer

The quality of local youth programs has a lot to do with the personalities and energy of those who run them. Most communities have activities for kids and teens, but how important are they to the local community overall? Do local leaders and parents regularly check in on the programs? Or do the programs run on their own without much outside input or supervision? Is your local government actively maintaining and renovating facilities for young people? Or does your local teen center still have avocado couches and brown shag carpeting?

As your family grows older, you will become part of a network of dads who have kids your children's ages who attend the same schools and participate with them in sports and other activities. Keep an ear to the local grapevine about what is happening in kids' programs and facilities, and make sure you are communicating with other parents about it. It is easy today to keep an ever-growing e-mail list of families whose kids share the same interests as yours and to contact them about opportunities to plug into new programs.

Your church, middle school, and high school groups should also become hubs of community development and care. There should be opportunities to engage kids and parents alike in volunteering to help others. Set an example for other dads in how to care for your community's youth.

worth thinking about

▶ Are you volunteering on at least one board of directors for a local nonprofit that organizes activities for youth? Doing so is a great way of living God's love in front of non-Christians.

▶ Read the local page of your city newspaper to keep up with what is happening around youth programs. Talk about these things with other parents in your church.

▶ Fatherlessness is a major issue for our communities today. What are you doing personally for kids who don't have dads at home?

> *A growing body of research points to the need to build the capacity of communities to support young people's healthy development as an integral part of society's alcohol, tobacco, and other drug prevention efforts.*
>
> Peter L. Benson

question

Do you know your neighbors?

Families are increasingly mobile these days, and they rarely live in the same community they grew up in, let alone the same neighborhood. As people find new jobs in new cities, they often find themselves settling into a collection of houses rather than a tightly knit and welcoming group of neighbors. However, if you want to build a caring safety net around your children, shouldn't you take the time to knock on some doors and introduce yourself?

answer

The term *neighbor* doesn't really mean what it used to. As households have become increasingly more self-sufficient and transitory—pulling the community together to bring in the harvest or raise a barn is pretty much a thing of the past—people have come to need their neighbors less and communicate with them even less than that. Neighbors don't watch out for one another the way they used to, and it is less common to know the person next door than those you work with who live an hour away.

If such barriers are to be broken, you have to actively find excuses to get to know your neighbors. You don't have to be new to a neighborhood to go knock on some doors. If you are moving into a community, look for neighborhoods where there are kids the same ages as yours. Make your home a neighborhood hangout for your kids and their friends.

As with any group of people, issues will come up. Just because the people next door have kids the same age as yours doesn't mean they will always get along or even that they hold the same values. Don't let this keep you from getting to know the people who live around you. Biblical principles speak specifically of blessing those around you even if it is not reciprocated. Getting to know your neighbors can be as much an opportunity to refine the love of God in you as it can be a help in time of need.

worth thinking about

▶ Consider going caroling at Christmastime or helping to organize a block barbecue around the Fourth of July. These can be great ways to break the ice with new neighbors.

▶ Grab your kids and go rake a neighbor's yard in the fall or clear their sidewalks of snow in winter, especially if you know it is a single parent or an elderly household.

▶ If your kids have a fund-raiser, go with them as they go door-to-door, and introduce yourself after your kids have made their appeal. Relationship building sets an example for your kids and can also help their fund-raising drives in the future!

Love your neighbor as yourself.
Mark 12:31, NIV

question

What other adults can your kids trust?

Who are the other adults in your kids' lives? Kids routinely rotate through teachers, coaches, and volunteers who work with their clubs and groups, but there are generally a handful of other parents and leaders who are around year after year. Have you invested the time to get to know these people? Are you building friendships with them as part of the support group for your kids as well as being a support to them?

answer

In an age of Internet predators and disappearing children, parents tend to be more suspicious than ever before of other adults who interact with their children—and certainly there is reason for caution. However, to isolate your kids from the influences of other adults and parents can be harmful in and of itself. Children need to hear a chorus of adult voices as they build their own value systems. If that chorus is absent or too diverse, you can find yourself in more clashes with your teen than you can handle.

A more threatening world should spur fathers to engage more with other adults in their kids' lives. There are a vast number of informative resources for parents today about those who prey on children. It would be foolish not to take advantage of them or to leave your kids in the care of any organization that doesn't do background checks, ask for references, or forbid adults from being alone with children. None of these, of course, can replace getting to know the adults your kids hang out with the most. Stay to watch practices every once in a while, attend open houses and family events, be friendly, and try to listen more than you talk when you interact with coaches, teachers, and other adult leaders.

worth thinking about

▶ Think of three things you would like your kids to get from relationships with other adults. Who are the adults you know from whom your kids might "catch" these characteristics?

▶ When you have the chance, see what the adults in your children's lives really know about your kids. See what insights they can provide on what your kids are like when you are not around.

▶ As kids graduate into middle school, they have fewer adults they can build quality relationships with for a number of reasons. Thus, as your kids get older, do more to encourage these relationships.

> *What really holds potential for making a moral impact on a mid-adolescent is a powerful connection with individual adults whom he can admire or idealize . . . who can inspire him to make moral sense of the social confusion of his surroundings.*
>
> Barbara Stilwell

Why should you seek wisdom?

It is a sad commentary of our times when our young must seek advice and counsel from "Dear Abby" instead of going to Mom and Dad.

Abigail Van Buren

56 question

Public, private, or homeschooling?

As our culture has become increasingly diverse, it seems schools have been the battleground for religious versus secular views and political correctness versus individual beliefs about morality, as well as the age-old versus new experimental teaching techniques. Considering all this, is it better to keep your kids home to educate them yourself, find a private school that shares your values and philosophies, or let your kids attend public schools that seem to be increasingly ineffective and more secular?

answer

Parents have good reasons to consider alternatives to public schooling these days, whether those reasons are based on a concern about conflicts with religious beliefs or about what would provide their children the best quality of education. Whether you have the time to be home with your kids during the day or the income to consider private schooling, you and every other parent need to consider the trade-offs in doing what is best for your children.

While the advantages of private schooling with smaller class sizes and specific curricula are obvious, the cost associated with private schooling is not feasible for everyone.

Meanwhile, homeschooling has grown in popularity and acceptance. Having the freedom to explore educational interests at your own pace, in light of what you believe and according to your child's own motivation, can produce amazing results.

Public schooling, however, lets your child be a witness, and it offers many programs and specialties you would not be able to provide at home. As a father, you need to weigh what will be best for your child's personality and abilities, and then be there to balance out the weaknesses of whatever educational model you and your wife choose.

worth thinking about

- ▶ **If you decide** to homeschool, find out about state laws for homeschooling regarding academic credit as well as homeschooling networks you can plug into in your area.

- ▶ **If you choose** to send your children to public or private school, talk with them regularly about what they are learning and how it affects their faith and the way they see the world.

- ▶ **Whichever of these** you choose for your kids, help them build a strong social network of friends who share their values. Participation in clubs and sports will go a long way toward achieving this.

> *Home schooling is not so much a rebellion against public schools as it is a choice made on social, academic, family, and religious grounds.*
> Chris Jeub

57

question

How often are you at their school?

If you choose to send your children to public or private school, how often are you around the school to get a feel for its atmosphere and what kids do there? Have you met the school administrators and your children's teachers? Are you there for games, concerts, parent-teacher conferences, and other activities and meetings? Are you part of the booster club or parent-teacher organization? Who is speaking for your values and beliefs in your school community?

answer

Every father should be known in the halls of his children's schools by administrators, teachers, coaches, and students. They need to know that they have your support in what they do—and that you respect their help in raising your children to be responsible and capable members of their classes, teams, and clubs. There is a high correlation between parent involvement in schools and the success of those schools in educating youth.

Do you know what your children are studying at school? Do you discuss those topics with your children as you help them with their homework? Great discussions about books, movies, and events in history are not just meant for the classroom; they're meant for the dinner table as well. Most textbooks gloss over the religious devotion of many of our greatest American heroes. Helping your children see this side of history can build a solid foundation for their faith as well as introduce the importance of using primary sources in any research. You can also help them develop the critical thinking skills they need.

Parent-teacher organizations too often become the breeding ground of political struggles fiercer than presidential elections. Don't hesitate to let your leadership skills be exercised in this arena.

worth thinking about

▶ **As you have** probably already seen, great dads have to be masters of time management. Are you passing these skills on to your children as they try to balance chores, homework, activities, and downtime?

▶ **Do you know** the other kids on your children's sports teams? Do you cheer as loudly for them as for your own kids? Take the opportunity at sporting events to get to know the parents of your children's friends.

▶ **Help your children** set high standards and goals for themselves. Your expectations will communicate what you think they are capable of. Never aim low.

> *Few will have the greatness to bend history itself, but each one of us can work to change a small portion of events, and in the total of all those acts will be written the history of this generation.*
> Robert F. Kennedy

question
▾
Does your community know your voice?

Who speaks for truth, integrity, and honesty in your city? Politics today have a horrible reputation for being corrupt and ruled by special-interest groups, but if no one is speaking for the interests of all, how will this ever change? Great dads are community leaders, whether in the church, neighborhood, city, or local youth programs. Do people in your community know who you are because you stand up and speak out for what is right?

answer
▾

The Bible says that a good father sits among the elders of the land and is known by the government of his city. This isn't necessarily because he runs for political office, but as issues touch his life and his family, he does not hesitate to stand up for what is right. He isn't afraid to make appointments with local officials or to organize presentations before the city council or county commission. He keeps a pulse on local politics and is willing to be involved where he can be.

In a similar way, more men should aspire to be elders and influencers in their churches—not for the sake of prestige, but in order to be examples of community servants who care about issues that affect the communities their churches touch. As overbooked as most men are simply earning a living for their families, this is no small commitment, but if good dads aren't willing to stand up and speak out, then by default more self-interested voices prevail.

Great dads don't shirk the responsibility of being leaders and influencers wherever they are involved. They set an example of civic responsibility for their children as well as enforce positive change in their neighborhoods. They speak up for quality youth programs, make sure the elderly are respected, and promote care for the needy as well as helping individuals be self-sustaining. Don't be shy about letting wisdom speak through you.

worth thinking about

▶ **A good place** to start this involvement is by volunteering for local civic events, political functions, or simply attending a local council or school board meeting.

▶ **How do you** keep informed about what is happening in your community, county, or state government? Do you talk about important issues with your family from time to time?

▶ **Never underestimate** the power of a single vote or a single voice. No matter what opposition you encounter at first, if you stand firm in living and speaking out on biblical principles, you will have an impact for good.

> *All that is necessary for the triumph of evil is that good men do nothing.*
> Edmund Burke

question

Do your kids make friends easily?

A huge part of any child's growing into a successful adult is mastering the world of social interaction. Kids need to know how to make friends who will support them and work together with them, people they can rely on and bounce thoughts off of, people who will help them stay the course and hold to their values no matter what is happening around them. Do your children have what it takes to build a support network of friends who share their values?

answer

Every father wants his kids to grow up to be responsible adults, but ensuring that is not something he can do all by himself. As kids graduate from middle school to high school and prepare for college, they will grow increasingly independent of you and their mother. Part of that separation will be turning to peers for feedback instead of you. High school can be a social minefield as adolescent immaturity meets adult decisions involving driving, dating, and morality.

Skills for making friends start as early as toddlers' learning to play together. It is all based on the balance of the Golden Rule—treat other people the way you would like other people to treat you. It is the balance between understanding the needs of the other person and your own. Play relationships often evolve into competitiveness and selfishness—one child always trying to get his or her way. Teaching sharing, taking turns, and kindness builds a foundation for future friendships.

As your kids grow older, you should watch their social patterns and be involved, but let your kids practice making decisions for themselves. Just because friends are neighbors doesn't mean they will be best friends for life. Watch your children's temperaments and help them discover when to give some friendships a time-out and when to develop new ones. Make sure your kids have good groups of kids to become friends with from your church youth group to clubs and sports.

worth thinking about

► **Try not to make** decisions about cutting off friendships without your kids' input, and don't let them cut off friendships without yours. Making these decisions together is an important learning process.

► **Just as with** siblings, don't intervene between your child and another child too quickly. Give them suggestions for solutions rather than directives.

► **Don't let kids** focus on the other person's actions alone. Help them learn that they have the power to avoid strife, even if it means choosing not to play with that child again for a while.

> *You use steel to sharpen steel,*
> *and one friend sharpens another.*
> Proverbs 27:17, The Message

60

Do your kids' friends know you?

Kids need to know that more than one set of parental eyes are watching out for them, and other parents need to know you are watching over their kids as you would your own. Are you a great dad to your kids' friends as well? When they see you after school or at the mall, do they stand up a little straighter and behave a little better?

answer

▼

There is no question that kids are influenced by their peers, and more often than not, if your children are coming home with new attitudes, it is the result of plugging in with some new friends. The first instinct of many parents is to try to keep bad influences away from their kids—and this can be a good idea if your child is much more of a follower than a leader—but to do so is also to miss the chance to teach your kids how to be a positive effect in a negative world.

All kids, including yours, are going to make mistakes, run into bullies, and be pressured to do things by their peers. This is to be expected and dealt with. But in what ways are you and your kids influencing those they interact with on a daily basis? This is much easier for them to do if they know you are there to support them. Your kids are also much less likely to have the wrong kinds of friends if they know they are expected to have them over to your home on a regular basis.

It is a sad statistic, but there are fewer and fewer kids who have a father's influence in their lives anymore. Being a "community dad" is much more important than it used to be. Kids that your children are around should know that you expect the best from and for them. Your influence in their lives might make all the difference in the world, so don't miss the opportunity to get to know them before you judge them.

worth thinking about

▶ God told Samuel to look at the heart, not the physical exterior. With today's odd fashions, oftentimes kids that look the roughest on the outside are the softest on the inside.

▶ As you pray for your kids, also pray for their friends and their friends' families. Get to know the parents of your kids' friends. Don't hesitate to call someone up and introduce yourself.

▶ Every once in a while have an event where you get together with the families of a group of your children's friends. It can be a great way to build a network of support.

> Keep open house; be generous with your lives. By opening up to others, you'll prompt people to open up with God, this generous Father in heaven.
> Matthew 5:16, THE MESSAGE

question

What happens if your children get in trouble at school?

Every father dreads the possibility of being called into the principal's office to discuss his son's or daughter's behavior or performance. The truth is, kids make mistakes and get into trouble from time to time, and sometimes your kids need help you would rather not acknowledge. What do you do if you are called in for a conference because your child got in a tussle with another child, is being a constant distraction in class, or is performing below expectations?

answer

Too often parents forget that teachers and administrators are part of society's network of adults to help them raise their children. It is easy to turn school into an "us versus them" scenario. Don't automatically defend your children, but work to help them grow. If you recognize that this is an opportunity for significant learning for your children instead of a mark against their character, such incidents can be wonderfully positive. Go in with an open mind looking for the best way to work together.

If your children are in trouble because of disciplinary problems, get all the facts. If you can, bring your children along to participate in at least part of the conference. Keep your children focused on what they could have done differently to avoid the problem rather than letting the blame be shifted elsewhere. If it is about performance, work on a plan with the teacher and your children to improve their grades.

Realize as well that somewhere in your children's education they are going to run into a teacher or two whom they don't get along with. Their personalities will clash, and you will have the opportunity to teach your children about respect for authority and getting along with different personality types. Never let your children doubt your confidence that they can solve these issues for themselves, nor let them doubt you will stand with them and support them through the entire time they have that teacher. You will both grow through the experience.

worth thinking about

- ▶ **Pray with your** children regularly for their principals, teachers, and coaches.

- ▶ **Let your children's** teachers know that you support them and appreciate all they are doing to help educate your children and prepare them for the future.

- ▶ **Teach your children** how to respectfully disagree but still stand strong in what they believe. Respect for authority does not mean forgetting what is right, and sometimes students have to unflinchingly stand for what they believe is true in high school and/or college.

> *One father is more than a hundred schoolmasters.*
> George Herbert

62 **question**

▼

Do your kids participate in sports and clubs?

As money gets tighter in school districts and homes, the first things that often get cut are the arts, clubs, and sports programs. Just how valuable is participating in such programs? With all the negative press about over-competitiveness in youth sports programs nowadays—not to mention the risk of injuries—is pushing your kids to be the best on the field really in their best interests for the long run?

answer

▼

While classroom work is a basic foundation for every child's future, too many underestimate the importance of extracurricular activities and nonacademic programs such as music, art, and athletics. While such things are outside what many consider the core educational subjects of reading, writing, and arithmetic, these other areas are where children learn about themselves and have the opportunity to discover their personal passions as they learn how to set goals and work hard to achieve them. Researchers emphasize that the socialization and self-confidence developed in participating in at least three hours a week of extracurricular sports or activities are an important factor in helping kids stay on track through adolescence and young adulthood.

There are, of course, some significant things to overcome along the way to make sure such experiences remain positive. An overemphasis on winning now rather than helping kids grow and develop as both individuals and athletes is more about adult egos than about helping kids grow into successful adults.

Great dads have to be part of the solution to keep things in perspective. As much as possible, let your children "play" sports and explore what they like to do. Their interests in these things—and your relationship with your kids—will benefit greatly down the road.

worth thinking about

▶ **Be a voice** for reason and sportsmanship on your child's sport teams. Just as a bad coach or loudmouthed parent can ruin such experiences, a reasonable, encouraging voice can make things better.

▶ **Kids develop** at different speeds, and the ones who develop the latest often tend to be the best athletes in high school. Keep things in perspective as your children grow.

▶ **Avoid letting** your kids quit something midseason, especially if it is because they feel they are not good enough. The determination to see it through will help build confidence in them.

Sports help children develop physical skills, get exercise, make friends, have fun, learn to play as a member of a team, learn to play fair, and improve self-esteem.
American Academy of Child and Adult Psychiatry

question

▼

Should you coach your children's teams?

There are few dads who have worse reputations than those who coach their children in sports. Either they are accused of playing favorites toward their own kids and their kids' friends, or they are seen as too hard on them, and their children eventually burn out. However, there are few things more rewarding than coaching your sons or daughters in a sport that you loved growing up as a kid. Considering the trade-offs, is it really worth it?

answer

▼

No dad should get into coaching without first being brutally honest with himself. Are you going to get too competitive? Will you lose your temper too easily? Do you understand that it is about having fun and not your win-loss record? Are you in it to help your kids grow more confident or to fulfill some part of your own life you feel you lost out on when you were younger? Do you have the knowledge to coach? Are you going to grow closer to your children through this activity or just grow more frustrated with one another?

The fact of the matter is that few youth sports programs would ever get off the ground without parent coaches. Volunteers are always needed, and chances are that if it isn't you, then it will be some other player's father. You certainly put yourself under the microscope when you volunteer to coach, but if you keep things positive, are organized, and communicate well with other parents, many problems will be defused before they arise. Plus, the younger the players, the more you can simply play everyone equally and emphasize the fun of the game.

As kids get older and skills and coaching ability become more of a factor, dads are still needed to help at practices, keep stats, manage car pools, and whatever else, but it is often wise to let more-experienced coaches take over at that point if they are available. By the time kids are in middle school, nonparent coaches are always best.

worth thinking about

▶ **If you are going** to coach, get another dad or two to coach with you. Work with his children and let him instruct yours. This can keep things more in the right perspective.

▶ **If you choose** not to coach, then don't. Being an obnoxious parent in the stands is worse than being an obnoxious coach on the sidelines.

▶ **Let your kids** start the discussions about their play and avoid the urge to overanalyze games in the car on the way home.

> *The most important thing . . . is not to win but to take part, just as the most important thing in life is not the triumph but the struggle. The essential thing is not to have conquered but to have fought well.*
>
> Olympic Creed

question

Do your children have a can-do attitude?

Great dads are all coaches for their kids—they help them develop their skills and self-discipline as well as their motivation and confidence in always doing their best whether they are tackling a difficult piano piece, a large homework project, or a fullback. Do your kids embrace challenges or back away from them? Do they have the skills to break a big responsibility down into bite-size pieces? Are they growing up into the type of person who can get things done?

answer

Self-confidence for children begins with their father's faith in them. It starts with the building of the first block tower and continues through graduation. Are you nurturing them to take on difficult assignments and be a leader? Do they know you believe they are capable of anything they dream they can do?

Kids tend to view issues passionately, but few have the drive to do anything about it. If you see your children concerned about the poor or homeless, sit down with them and ask them what they think would make a difference. Encourage them to raise money for a local shelter, write local government officials, or start a drive to collect blankets in the winter. It doesn't matter what they do, but don't let them get excited and not do something about it. The more they accomplish, the more they will believe they can accomplish. Put their enthusiasm to work.

Should they have a difficult goal before them like winning a student council election or improving their shooting percentage, sit down with them and help develop objective steps to accomplishing their goals. Then offer whatever help you can in encouraging them through each step. Having a can-do attitude starts with making a plan and then doing something about it. Look for opportunities to encourage your kids in this area—you will be surprised by what they can accomplish!

worth thinking about

▶ **Giving kids** age-appropriate chores will help your kids appreciate a job well done.

▶ **Encourage your children** to participate in their student council or the leadership of their youth group. Learning to plan and carry out activities develops the skills necessary to be a person who can get things done.

▶ **Rudimentary goal-setting** and decision-making skills are important to accomplishing any dream or desire. Help your kids develop these from a young age.

> *We need a renaissance of wonder. We need to renew, in our hearts and in our souls, the deathless dream, the eternal poetry, the perennial sense that life is miracle and magic.*
>
> E. Merrill Root

65

▼

Where does wisdom come from?

It goes with the territory that great dads should always offer great advice, but where do you get it? Does insight just come from living more years on the planet, or are there sources where you can go and search it out? What is wisdom anyway? How can you make sure you are getting wiser as you get older and not just fooling yourself? When your kids come to you asking for advice, how do you know what you have to say will really help?

answer

▼

At its simplest, wisdom is the art of making good life decisions. One of the most slippery things about wisdom is its simplicity. The Bible says that wisdom sits all day crying in the streets and marketplaces to be received, but no one hears it. For the average man, wisdom could walk up and shake his hand and he wouldn't know it.

Why? Because, as a rule, wisdom seems too simple to be relevant. Wisdom is disregarded from the start because the hearer is blinded by knowing better himself. He has a solution or plan that fits the situation like a glove, whereas the wisdom offered would take too much work or cause too much trouble. Why be honest, for example, when a little white lie can be told and no one will notice?

Men are blind to wisdom because of their pride, laziness, and selfishness. Then when everything crashes down around their shoulders, they look back and wonder how they could have been so stupid.

In truth, wisdom is all around. It is certainly in the Bible, but also in other books that give you knowledge to handle your work, home, and future. It is crying out in the stories and lives of those around you. It is calling to you in the wee hours of the morning when you should be praying over your day instead of checking the league standings for the umpteenth time in the sports section. If you are humble enough to seek it, you will easily find it—but you do have to actively look.

worth thinking about

▶ **The Book of Proverbs** is broken up into thirty-one chapters—basically one chapter for each day of the month. Take a month to read it, and see what happens. Many who have tried this have been reading and rereading Proverbs for years.

▶ **Wisdom doesn't** puff you up, but it encourages and enlightens. True wisdom always humbles you and makes you open to more wisdom.

▶ **Wisdom is also** caught from others. Who are the wise men around you? They are rarely the flashiest or most outgoing; they are simply those whose lives just seem to work.

> *Wisdom is supreme; therefore get wisdom.*
> *Though it cost all you have, get understanding.*
> Proverbs 4:7, NIV

Do your kids really watch everything you do?

I watched a small man with thick calluses on both hands work fifteen and sixteen hours a day. I saw him once literally bleed from the bottoms of his feet, a man who came here uneducated, alone, unable to speak the language, who taught me all I needed to know about faith and hard work by the simple eloquence of his example.

Mario Cuomo

66

question

How do you plant wisdom in your children?

Wisdom is best received when it is sought after—it is most cherished when it is sipped from the ladle by the same person who dropped the bucket down the well and cranked it up himself. Wisdom, by its very nature, cannot be inflicted upon others. It can be found only by those who look for it. How then, if they have to seek it out for themselves, can you plant wisdom in your children?

answer

Wisdom is a lot like sunscreen—you generally don't realize you should have applied it until you are already burned. In other words, for your children to learn to choose to seek wisdom before it is too late, they need to understand that there are consequences to their actions, and that bad consequences often can be avoided by first seeking out advice. It is a tough lesson to learn as self-will and self-certainty distort their point of view.

Don't shelter your children from the consequences of their actions when the costs are small. Help them understand how a different course would have had different results. Always administer discipline with compassion. Let your children know that you love them and cannot go along with their actions because their attitude is willful rather than self-controlled. As your kids grow older, hold them responsible for getting their work done. They should have a way to earn money and pay for their own things as well as their own mistakes. If they break a window or dent the car, let them pay for it. It may seem an expensive lesson, but it is much less costly when they are in grade school than when they are in college.

If you can lovingly counsel them rather than be the judge and jury, then they will understand your voice as one of wisdom. When you become a source of advice rather than condemnation, you can be confident wisdom is taking root in their hearts.

worth thinking about

- ▶ Teach your children about wisdom and read to them from Proverbs when they are young. As they get older, the Book of Ecclesiastes may be more appropriate—it is written as if it were a thesis on life for college students.

- ▶ Wisdom is difficult to receive when the hearer is on the defensive.

- ▶ We know that David planted wisdom in Solomon's heart because when Solomon was young and God went to him, his request was for not power or wealth, but wisdom. What were David's characteristics that he was able to do this?

> *Parents are not the only voice in your children's ear, so you better be the best voice, the clearest voice, the most influential voice in your children's ear.*
>
> Jay McGraw

67 question

How do you teach right from wrong?

The Bible says that foolishness is bound up in the heart of a child—children don't yet understand that nothing right can happen from doing something wrong. Children, from the time they can walk, will start experimenting with ways to get what they want, often choosing the easy and direct way rather than the conscientious one. How do you instill in them the desire to do what is right?

answer

Regardless of what many modern philosophers believe, while children do come into the world innocent—free of the evil taught in our society—they do not come into the world "good." It is a strange paradox, but human beings come into the world with a natural inclination to watch out for "number one"—themselves—and this self-importance and self-promotion are the basis for all the wrong things they will do in their lives. Jesus gave two commandments: make God "number one" instead of yourself, and balance all your wants and desires with the wants and desires of others (i.e., love other people in the same way you love yourself).

This is why you don't punish kids for making mistakes—though you do hold them accountable to the consequences—but you do punish children for rebellion, disobedience, and acting selfishly. Blatant displays of self-will should never be rewarded. You need to stand strong for them to rethink their tactics. There will be times in the heat of such battles when your calm silence will be more effective than a spanking—great dads rarely lose their cool.

Kids learn right and wrong from not being overindulged and from learning to respect the rights and desires of others. If you can stand strong in this while your kids are young, the lesson will be permanently ingrained in them.

worth thinking about

▶ **You are going** to make some mistakes in disciplining your kids, and there will be times they teach you instead of the other way around. Never be afraid to apologize to your kids or give them a big hug for doing better than you would yourself.

▶ **If you are** to be able to discipline your children correctly as well as be a proper model for them, you must start by guarding your own heart. Start each day submitting yourself to the Lord and asking for His strength to live right.

▶ **It is better to let** your kids learn from your mistakes than their own. Be humble.

> *Principle—particularly moral principle—can never be a weathervane, spinning around this way and that with the shifting winds of expediency. Moral principle is a compass forever fixed and forever true.*
> Edward R. Lyman

question
▼

How do you teach your children to think?

While you want your children to be obedient and not get in trouble at home or at school, you don't want them to be puppets, either, always controlled by others and the flow of popular opinion. However, in order to have the conviction to stand up for what is right no matter what anyone else says, kids need to be able to think for themselves and come to correct conclusions. How do you challenge your kids to think for themselves?

answer
▼

As your children navigate middle school, their cognitive functions will begin to develop to new levels, and the age of reason (though, unfortunately, not reasonableness) will begin to dawn for them. With this new level of analysis will come the ability to think for themselves, the two-edged sword that enables them to become self-sustaining individuals who question everything you ever told them was true.

If you have already established a healthy thirst for wisdom and a solid understanding of good and evil in your kids, then you've given them a solid foundation toward figuring things out for themselves. When that cognitive switch goes off in their brains that what they were just told does not fit the view of the world they grew up with, how are you going to be sure they come back down on the side of what you've taught them was true?

To be honest, you really can't, but you can hedge the field in your favor if you are willing to walk them through issues before they come to decisions that are earth-shattering. On things they state as absolutes they hear at school, question them and see how they do under some light cross-examination. If you never take the time to challenge them when they are young, you may not be up to the task of defending your position when they challenge you!

worth thinking about

▶ **Don't let mealtime** discussion be about only how everyone's day was. From time to time discuss current events and challenge deeper thinking about them.

▶ **How did you come** to believe what you believe? What is your worldview based upon? If you are not sure about this, you may want to do some research of your own before your kids put such questions to you.

▶ **Does your church** have basic classes in exploring its tenets of faith? If not, get with your pastor and see about starting one for adolescents and adults alike.

> *Don't be gullible. Check out everything,*
> *and keep only what's good. Throw*
> *out anything tainted with evil.*
> 1 Thessalonians 5:21–22, The Message

question

How do you teach them to love knowledge?

Do your children love learning? Do they like school? Kids tend to think of school as something done to them rather than as an opportunity to stretch their wings and explore the universe and expand their limits. While school is a place that is supposed to prepare them for life, too many kids go there resenting it rather than grateful for the opportunities it presents. How can you pass on a healthy thirst for knowledge to your kids?

answer

To begin with, how is your thirst for knowledge? When you become a father yourself, there are a lot of things about your childhood that suddenly look different. It is not uncommon for self-made multimillionaires who never finished eighth grade to insist their kids attend college through a master's program. Is that a double standard? No, it is just that they now know the value of a good education—it is something you should never let your children neglect, either.

Primarily your kids will catch a thirst for knowledge from you. Do you ask about what they learned at school? What are they reading? Is it a book you have read and loved? When you have free time, are you expanding what you know and getting better at something, or are you vegging out in front of the television?

Find out what your kids are interested in, and feed that interest. Take them to museums or the library and research with them. A love for learning in general usually starts with specializing in one topic first, and then letting the research you do in that area serve as a springboard for learning later in life. Loving to learn is really a discipline that becomes a habit. It is a passion that leads to diligence. It is best caught when your kids are young and just learning to read. Take the time to learn with your kids, and they will come to love it.

worth thinking about

- ▶ **Before you go** on your next campout, get a map of the stars and constellations to take with you. See if you can find them in the sky and then see if you can find the stories that inspired the names of the constellations.

- ▶ **Take your own** field trip to a pond or creek near your house. Bring along a magnifying glass, and take samples home to put under a microscope.

- ▶ **Buy a bird** or bug book of creatures in your area and see if you can identify them as you drive around or go on walks together.

> *Children need models rather than critics.*
> Joseph Joubert

70

question

▼

How do you teach them to value truth?

One has but to open a browser these days to the average home page to get more information than most people could gather in a week a century ago. But is the world better for all the information available with a few taps on a keyboard? How do you sift all the information from the disinformation? How much is just white noise, and how much is really making your kids better people?

answer

▼

It is important to teach your children the difference between knowledge and wisdom as well as facts and truth. Knowledge is understanding facts about something; wisdom is knowing how to correctly apply knowledge—or knowing what to do in a specific situation. Facts are individual bits of information; truth is the sum of spiritual principles and natural laws that govern the whole. Facts have to be interpreted through truth. Too often, however, facts are used to try to build overarching theories or laws that pretend to be truth but are ultimately false.

The science-versus-religion debate is a good example of this confusion. Science takes individual facts and tries to make statements about the nature of the universe through them. Atheists take these facts from the natural world and try to apply them to the spiritual universe to justify their "truth" that God doesn't exist, but they are postulating beyond the realm of what the facts state.

Great dads will teach their kids to distinguish between the true and the false as well as to keep digging for deeper truths. Even biblical truths need to be mined to understand all that is in them. The church should be an encourager of real science and research, not an opponent. Psychologists are now starting to reinforce the virtues taught in the Bible as the best way to live healthy, fulfilling lives, whereas a few decades ago they were challenging them. It may take some time, but in the end, the truth will always win out.

worth thinking about

▶ **Mythology and parables** are about teaching truth; history is about teaching facts. As such, the Bible is a historically accurate myth—God writing truth in human history. There has never been an archaeological find that contradicted what is recorded in the Bible.

▶ **No matter what** they are studying, always encourage your kids to keep digging. True science began with Christians' wondering at God's creation and how it works—it is for your children to take that questioning to the next level.

▶ **Love is the** ultimate truth—a philosophical system that promotes self over others is ultimately false.

> *Embrace truth! Love peace!*
> Zechariah 8:19, The Message

question

▼

Do your kids have chores and responsibilities?

With kids busier than ever these days, many parents feel that expecting them to do anything more than their homework may be too much. Why should kids need to do the dishes or mow the lawn if the parents have time to do it? Is there any intrinsic value in kids' doing chores and having responsibilities around the house? Do parents really have the right to make their kids do things they never liked to do themselves?

answer

▼

As a great dad, turning your family into a team that works together and supports one another is a primary part of your job description. Certainly that means getting along with one another and keeping peace in the home, but it also means contributing to the overall welfare and cleanliness of the home. There is nothing wrong with kids' doing chores; in fact, it is good for them to feel that they are contributing to the overall success of the family.

That said, however, chores need to be reasonable and fitting to the age of the child. As in everything, you need to be the leading example in doing them. The best way is to make a list of all the chores that need to be done and have a family meeting to negotiate who will do what.

Don't be afraid to include things like paying the rent and driving kids to lessons (after all, you do work for a living, and these chores should count for something as well).

Then hold to the standard and inspect what you expect. If you have a rule that the house will be clean before the television is turned on, then hold to it and be a leader in getting things straightened up. If you expect your kids to pick up after themselves, then make sure you pick up your things in the living room and take your plates and put them in the dishwasher after meals. The habits they form when your kids are young will last them a lifetime!

worth thinking about

▶ **For young children,** having a chart for family chores and keeping their rooms clean and clothes picked up works great. Have them put their own stickers on the chart, and have a standard for how many stickers need to be accumulated for "privilege status" on the weekend.

▶ **Make chores** as specific as possible. "No toys or clothes on the floor and bed made" is better than "Keep your room clean."

▶ **Try to group** chores so that everyone is working at the same time and done at the same time.

> *I often think today of what an impact could be made if children believed they were contributing to a family's essential survival and happiness. In the transformation from a rural to an urban society, children are . . . robbed of the opportunity to do genuinely responsible work.*
>
> Dwight D. Eisenhower

question

How do you introduce them to Jesus?

Every Christian parent wants their children to come to know Jesus for themselves. Meeting Christ is not so much learning a philosophy for living as it is coming to the knowledge of who Jesus is and what He has done for them. Do your kids believe that God raised Jesus from the dead, and do they accept Him as the Lord of their lives and their Savior from their sins? If not, how do you introduce them to salvation through Jesus Christ?

answer

Start with what you know. How did you come to Christ? How old were you when you met Him? How did you know the experience was genuine? If you can answer these questions, then you have a blueprint for your kids. Start with where you are and work from there.

Be patient. If you want your children to have a genuine experience with Christ, you can't force it; you can only lay the groundwork for it. Pray that your kids will be open to the truth and that they will recognize it when it is presented. Make sure you are attending church regularly where the gospel is presented in Sunday school. Talk with your kids about what God is doing in your life and how you know He is real. Do your homework, and be ready to answer their questions, but at the same time don't be afraid to say you don't know and will get back to them later. Live Christ before them. Love them as Jesus would. Develop the fruit of the Spirit in your life, and let them know that following Jesus is the greatest adventure a person can live.

When they come to Jesus, don't get lax. Coming to Christ may start with a one-time decision, but it is also something you have to do afresh every morning before you step out into the world. Know that their childish faith will have to grow, just as yours does.

worth thinking about

▶ **If someone** came to you and told you they wanted to become a Christian, what would you tell them? What scriptures would you show them, and what would you pray with them?

▶ **The older** your children are when you begin, the longer it may take them to come to Christ and the less likely you will be able to lead them to Jesus yourself. Make sure they are attending camps and meetings where they can hear the gospel from others as well as you.

▶ **Read and discuss** the Gospels with your kids before they go to bed and night. Mark is an easy one to start with for smaller kids; John might be more appropriate for teens.

> *I have been reminded of your sincere faith, which first lived in your grandmother Lois and in your mother Eunice and, I am persuaded, now lives in you also.*
> Paul to Timothy, 2 Timothy 1:5, NIV

73

question

▼

How do you live your faith before them?

How "Christian" do you think your kids would say that you are? It is one thing to accept Jesus and go to church regularly, but another to follow Jesus in front of them all the time. What are you like at work and with friends? Do your kids know the story of how you came to Jesus? Do they see the results of your prayer life? Do they regularly hear you talking about what it means to follow Jesus?

answer

▼

The key is not merely living your faith in front of your kids—it is living your faith everywhere. Then the second step is taking the time to be with your kids a lot. It is as simple and as difficult as that.

Of course, living as a Christian these days takes considerable initiative. You need to constantly encourage yourself in Christ and challenge and build your faith. The Bible says that faith works by love, and that the only way to show your faith to others is through the good works your faith inspires you to do. Do your kids see you tithing? Do they see you volunteering at church and in your community? Do they see your faith reflected in what you watch on television, where you surf on the Internet, in the books you read and the movies you watch? Do they see you meeting with other fathers and being accountable to one another to keep your faith on course? Do you read the Bible and pray each day? Does what comes out of your mouth reflect the grace that is in your heart?

Make sure you attend a church that challenges your faith and how you live as well as provides opportunities for you to serve. Make sure that it has solid youth programs and that the ministers are people you can meet with who will encourage you. Live Christianity as the adventure it is, and your kids won't be able to resist it.

worth thinking about

▶ **Faith is a mixture** of conviction, good works, and trusting God to see that all you set your hand to will have His mark upon it. How are you building these into your life?

▶ **Your relationship** with God is built on the same thing that your relationship with your child is—time. How are you spending time with God?

▶ **There is a part** of praising and worshiping God that happens in church services, and another that happens in the way you live every moment of your life. Live in a way that praises God.

> *It is my hope that my son, when I am gone, will remember me not from the battle field but in the home repeating with him our simple daily prayer, "Our Father who art in Heaven."*
>
> Douglas MacArthur

question

Can your kids defend what they believe?

Most children of Christians come to Jesus when they are in elementary school and seem to just "live their parents' faith" into their teens or college years. As your kids grow older, can they explain why they believe as they do with answers they have reasoned out themselves, or do they simply offer rote answers they are parroting from Sunday school lessons? Have you helped them use their critical thinking skills to be able to defend their faith?

answer

Recent statistics suggest that 75 percent to 85 percent of kids graduating from high school go on to lose their faith at college because they can't defend what they believe in the increasingly Christian-hostile academic world. The authority of Scripture no longer holds sway, and rules of logic and truth are no longer adhered to. If you want your kids to hold on to their faith into adulthood, then you need to make sure they are ready to defend every aspect of their beliefs before they leave home.

Your kids need to understand that persuasive arguments and words are poor foundations for truth—the worlds of theory and practice always collide. What sounds good and right in a discussion may not prove true in practice. At the same time, some things may have the desired result, but the method is flawed and harmful. The ends do not justify the means. The Bible says to judge all philosophical systems and teachings by their fruit.

There is no end-all argument for what Christians believe, but there is also no better witness of God than what Christians do. There are few, if any, atheist orphanages, and most hospitals and universities were started as Christian organizations. God is best seen in the people who use His love to change lives. Ground your children in that principle as well as solid apologetics.

worth thinking about

▶ **The Book of James** says that Christians are to show their faith in the good things they do, and that what a person believes without putting it into action is meaningless. Look for opportunities to let your faith touch the lives of others.

▶ **There are several** good resources available for helping defend Christianity in a debate. Talk with your pastor about what he would suggest.

▶ **Teach your kids** about the limits of scientific argument and philosophy alone as a way of discovering truth. Intellectually honest people will recognize the limits of these systems of thought and analysis in determining the spiritual nature of the universe.

> *If someone asks about your Christian hope, always be ready to explain it.*
> 1 Peter 3:15, NLT

question

How do you develop resiliency in your child?

Resiliency is the attribute that helps your kids bounce back from failures and stay the course of their dreams, avoiding the pitfalls of adolescence and the criticism of others. It is an inner drive that gets a person out of bed in the morning and on time to school despite whatever the world throws at them. How do you develop this in your kids? How do you help them develop this kind of resistance to setbacks?

answer

Resiliency is a slippery thing in kids. Where two kids in the same family may face the same bad circumstances in life—the death of a parent or being taken from parents because of drug use or imprisonment—one child will become self-destructive and the other will become responsible. The first may become a rebel who is always in trouble. The second may become a model student who gets his brothers and sisters up plus himself and ready for school on time and will balance all that with a part-time job to help pay the bills. There is no question that strong families make a difference in the well-being of kids. When the chips are down, however, how can you be sure your kids will push through rather than merely fold under the pressure?

Resilient kids are problem solvers who show an ability to adapt to various circumstances and keep a positive attitude and a good sense of humor in the midst of them. They have strong communications and social skills. They also have a strong sense of purpose that can stand up to adversity and oppression from outside sources, whether in an environment that is hostile to their beliefs or race or even in a war zone.

These kids have their lives built on the rock of their faith and calling in life. Complacency is not part of their makeup. Look for ways to model these characteristics and to build them into the lives of your kids.

worth thinking about

▶ **According to research**, there are three main contributors to resiliency in kids: supportive relationships; high, positive expectations; and opportunities for meaningful participation in their communities.

▶ **Low expectations** for kids—primarily in adolescents—feed complacency and poor behavior. Are you challenging your kids to make a difference and contribute to their society? To your family?

▶ **Pray with your kids** on a regular basis about what God's calling and purpose is for their lives.

> *Anyone who hears and obeys these teachings of mine is like a wise person who built a house on solid rock. Rain poured down, rivers flooded, and winds beat against that house. But it did not fall, because it was built on solid rock.*
> Matthew 7:24–25, CEV

▼

Where do children learn about responsibility to be their best?

▼

Father taught us that opportunity and responsibility go hand in hand. I think we all act on that principle; on the basic human impulse that makes a man want to make the best of what's in him and what's been given him.

Laurence Rockefeller

76

question

Are your kids impacting their world?

Are your kids learning to live their faith? In the face of intellectual attacks on Christianity, there may be no greater argument for the power of God's love than those who take it to the streets in helping and serving others. Do your kids believe they can make a difference in an increasingly depressed and selfish world? What are they doing to act on those beliefs and make a difference in other people's lives?

answer

You don't have to dig too deeply into history to find out that a lot of great figures started doing important things in their teen years. George Washington was already a surveyor for the state of Virginia. At twenty-two he was appointed a lieutenant colonel of its militia and led troops in the French and Indian Wars. Abraham Lincoln spent his teens educating himself well enough to become a lawyer. At fourteen, Leonardo da Vinci was already apprenticed as an artist. These men all found their callings at young ages. At twelve, Jesus was amazing people with His teachings.

Today society acts as if being a child is completely separate from growing up. Kids are encouraged to "just be kids" as long as possible, and the trend is encouraging immaturity well into college and beyond. It is as if kids can goof around most of their lives and then just transform into competent adults in their twenties.

Find opportunities for your kids to find a passion and purpose in helping others, and be involved. Infuse them with the confidence that youth is not a disadvantage, but that they should be examples of integrity in how they speak, how they carry themselves, how they care for others, and how they relate to God. Expect excellence and encourage them in their service. They will thrive through their contributions.

worth thinking about

- ▶ **Purposeless kids** generally "have fun" at the expense of others. Purpose-filled kids have fun serving others. Your kids need to know the difference.

- ▶ **American society** today instills youth with little more than the dream of growing up to live wealthy, comfortable lives. What aspirations are you instilling in your kids?

- ▶ **It is easy** to become overwhelmed by all the needs in the world. Help your kids find focus through purpose and what God puts on their hearts.

> *Build me a son whose heart will be clean, whose goal will be high; a son who will master himself before he seeks to master other men. . . . Give him humility, so that he may always remember the simplicity of greatness, the open mind of true wisdom, the meekness of true strength.*
>
> Douglas MacArthur

77

question
▼
What happened to your sweet little children?

There is no question about it, but something powerful happens when kids are near the age of thirteen. The only thing more shocking than their changing bodies is the way their attitudes toward you change. It was one thing when they defied you at ten and you hauled them to their room for discipline, but what do you do now with a teen who is standing nose-to-nose with you? Why the Jekyll-and-Hyde transformation?

answer
▼
Adolescence is a time of change. The hope is that your children will enter it with innocence and leave it with the savvy they need to face the world on their own, but the voyage from twelve into adulthood is anything but a straight trip from point A to point B. For most kids, seventh grade is a "sproing!" year—it is like a big spring releases inside of them, and whatever values, habits, and interpersonal skills weren't nailed down firmly will go flying in every direction. The rest of adolescence is about picking them up and putting them back together.

The good news is that researchers all agree there is primarily one factor that tells whether or not your kids will navigate adolescence successfully without getting caught in any of its risky behavior tide pools or getting grounded on any of its rocky attitudes: caring and involved parents.

Adolescence is the time when you and your kids realize they won't be living with you forever. Teens need to have an anchor they can depend on through such times. If you can be that steadying force for them—being calm when they are losing it and guiding them gently back to reality—adolescence can be the time in which you realize they really can do it on their own.

worth thinking about

▶ **There has been a good** deal of new research about the changes taking place in kids during their teen years. The results of this research can help you understand what they are going through and keep you more emotionally steady through what too many see as unmanageable times.

▶ **Teaching kids** self-control, respect for authority, and critical thinking when they are younger can make the teen years much easier on you as a father.

▶ **No matter** what happens with your adolescent children, imitate Jesus. Be the rock that stands firm, the rock they can depend upon to hold to what is right.

> *Your defining act of love for your child will not be the 2:00 AM feeding, the sleepless, fretful night spent beside him in the hospital, or the second job you took to pay for college. Your zenith will occur in the face of a withering blast of frightful rage from your adolescent, in allowing no rage from yourself in response. Your finest moment may well be your darkest. And you will be a parent.*
>
> Michael J. Bradley

question

How do you reason with their unreasonableness?

Teenagers certainly have a reputation in today's culture for exasperating their parents. In the battle between passion and reason, too often passion seems to take the day. What do you do when your adolescents want to engage in a knock-down, drag-out fight about something you know is morally, ethically, or legally wrong? When they stand strong defending something you see as indefensible, how do you get them to come back around to reason?

answer

Adolescence is about budding adults' changing their minds—literally. Recent studies show the brain changes more during the years between thirteen and twenty-five than any other period outside of the womb. The brain is housecleaning; it is replacing the neural pathways and rote instincts of childhood with the cognitive and analytical abilities of adulthood. As intellects emerge to see the world in all the colors of the rainbow rather than in just black and white, teens question everything they believed up to this point. They wonder if it will all fit in their awakening new perspective.

Do not fall into the trap of being heatedly entangled in disagreements. No matter how passionate your kids get, a great deal of that passion is a result of where they are in life. Keep in mind that the reasoning ability in their brains is being rewired and that it occasionally goes "off-line."

As your kids are "making up their minds," they need you to stick to your beliefs more than ever before. It is not uncommon for a father to hear his child arguing with friends, defending the same side of an argument the dad had expressed in a debate a few days before, even though he was certain he hadn't been convincing. Your kids will always be more like you than they are ever willing to admit.

worth thinking about

- ▶ Make sure you lay a foundation for reasonable debate during preteen years.

- ▶ What do you truly believe? Be prepared to defend your perspective coolly even in the heat of an argument.

- ▶ You want your children to be independent thinkers who can stand up for their values. Take the initiative to present questions of social justice or spark a conversation about current events yourself from time to time.

> When I was a boy of fourteen, my father was so ignorant I could hardly stand to have the old man around. But when I got to be twenty-one, I was astonished at how much he had learned in seven years.
>
> Mark Twain

79

question

How do you deal with rebellion?

As two-year-olds are infamous for their tantrums, teens are known for their open rebellion to their parents and other authority figures. From the way they wear their hair to what they put through their noses and what comes out of their mouths, teens give parents reason to fear adolescence. How should you deal with such acts of "individuality"? Is it just a phase to be tolerated that your kids will grow out of, or is it something you need to confront and conquer?

answer

While rebellion isn't pretty at any age, it can be down-right dangerous when kids reach their teens. When rebellion is mixed with bigger, stronger bodies able to reproduce, drive, and have access to money to purchase anything from beer to drugs to pornography, the results can be devastating. Rebellion is the epitome of foolishness because it replaces all authority with self-will and blinds teens to their need for God or wisdom. It is making a god out of self.

This is one reason why dealing with rebellion in smaller doses when children are younger is important. For one, the stakes are much lower when they are younger, and if needed, you can still throw them over your shoulder and take them to their room. It is also a reason to model reasonableness with them while disciplining them when they are younger—if you model stomping out the door and slamming it behind you, why should you expect them to do anything different when they have car keys in their pocket?

Yet you need to realize that you are still in the position of authority, and there are ways for you to deal with their rebellion. Let them know that while they may be against you, you are not against them, but that if they won't listen to you, then privileges stop.

worth thinking about

▶ **The Book of James** says that what comes out of a person's mouth tends to steer their actions. If you set a standard of only speaking respectfully to each other when they are small, a great deal of the bite can be taken out of rebellion when your kids get older.

▶ **Don't be surprised** if your kids have learned how to push your emotional buttons by the time they are preteens, if not before. Begin to practice not getting dragged into arguments when they are young.

▶ **Lying and deceit** are forms of rebellion. Model telling the truth and keeping your word no matter the cost, and expect your kids to do the same.

> *Rebelling against God or disobeying him because you are proud is just as bad as worshiping idols or asking them for advice.*
> 1 Samuel 15:23, CEV

question

Are your kids excited about their future?

As a rule, teenagers are known for their angst—a general dread or anxiety about the future because of its myriad of choices and uncertainty. In modern society this leads to everything from depression to drug and alcohol abuse. High schools today actually have higher levels of depression than psychiatric wards did in the 1950s! Yet it doesn't have to be that way. How can you infect your kids not just with hope for the future but also with excitement about it?

answer

There is an old saying that if you don't stand for something, you will fall for anything. This seems a great description of America's teenagers today. Their crisis of purpose is feeding an age of meaninglessness and disillusionment. They seem to see nothing but an endless sameness to their future and so live only for the moment. Many of them make poor decisions that will affect the rest of their lives.

The rewiring of cognitive functions of the brain during adolescence has several effects, but one of the most significant is that teens don't see the connection between today's actions and tomorrow's consequences. Rational thought does not kick in and say, "Riding my skateboard off the roof and onto the trampoline to see if I can launch myself into the pool might not end the way I envision it." This is not an excuse for their actions, but you do need to force your kids to slow down and think things through; rational thought does not come naturally for them.

As you are working with your kids to find their purpose in life, you constantly have to get them to visualize what their futures hold and to be motivated by it. They need to get excited about where they are going, what they are going to do, and how they are going to impact the world.

worth thinking about

▶ **Among the current** events you share at the dinner table, talk about the human-interest stories of people doing good things to help others. Discuss how you as a family can do similar things.

▶ **Celebrate the simple** joys of life: friends, family time, good work, and interesting conversation. While life can be full of lofty goals, happiness is built on quality relationships and doing the task at hand well.

▶ **Take time to help** your kids make the big decisions of college and career. Get them to start thinking about them early and give them plenty of time. Help them develop good life goals.

> *The grand essentials to happiness in this life are something to do, something to love, and something to hope for.*
> Joseph Addison

question

What should you tell them about sex?

Today's culture has told adolescents they are still children even though physically they can do anything adults can. For many this has turned sexual activity from something shared between married adults into experimentation and a game among teens. Yet the ramifications of premature sexual activity are often life altering. What should you be telling your teens about sex? How can you be sure they will wait until marriage?

answer

Whether your dad did or not, it is primarily your job to have "the talk" with your sons—moms, of course, can handle the details with daughters, but you also need to let your daughters know the male perspective as well. No matter how uncomfortable it is—and there are now a lot of resources out there to make it more comfortable—the first thing you need to do is resolve that you will not leave this responsibility to others.

Take time to get away from your normal life for a weekend, and let your son know it is to talk about some important issues concerning relationships and sex. They will not be as unwilling to do this as you might think (or as you are!). Get some good resources and prepare yourself to discuss these things professionally, but at the same time have fun with it.

The mistakes you may have made in this area do not disqualify you from urging your kids to save sex for marriage. If you made mistakes, then you know why you want something different for your kids—if you did not, then you know the joy of having the first and only person you've shared sex with be your wife. Don't let your kids miss out on the best!

worth thinking about

▶ **Help your kids** understand the overpowering pull sex has on human beings. Urge them to stay as far away from compromising situations as they can. Self-control in this area is not about seeing how close you can get without falling in.

▶ **Helping kids** understand what love truly is when it is healthy is a good way to keep sexual needs in perspective. Proper hugs and snuggles at home will help keep your kids from seeking such affection in the wrong places.

▶ **Make sure** your kids have space to ask whatever questions they would like while you are away for "the talk" weekend. It will be the most comfortable time for them to do it, and they will be more open later if you let them be more open during that time.

If you try to establish intimacy with another person before achieving a sense of identity on your own, all of your relationships become an attempt to complete yourself.

Les Parrott

question

▼

What do you tell them about dating?

In a society that now associates "going out" with "hooking up" and considers casual sex as having "friends with benefits," what should you be teaching your teen about dating? Can you help your kids avoid not only the pitfalls of premarital sex but also the emotional turmoil that goes with today's adolescent culture of "going steady" and "breaking up" before they even learn how to make friends of the opposite sex?

answer

▼

There is good reason to question what society has done to teenagers in this day and age. Before the turn of the twentieth century, when children reached the age of thirteen they didn't become adolescents, they became adults. They went to work, they got married, and they became responsible as contributors to society. Over the last century, these kids became teenagers—a new phase of life caught between adulthood and childhood, and suddenly no one was responsible for growing up so fast anymore. Teens were turned from contributors to consumers, and the expectations of these fully grown children were lowered from doing honest work to barely keeping their rooms cleaned.

Most of the time dating is no big deal, but the one time you make a mistake, the results can be life changing.

Don't let your teens be eager to date. Set strict limits on their dating until you feel they are mature enough to keep themselves out of potentially compromising situations. Encourage them, however, to take advantage of opportunities to develop friendship and communication skills in relating to the opposite sex in healthy environments where they are chaperoned. Youth groups, social gatherings in your home, or volunteering together in your community are great opportunities for this.

worth thinking about

▶ **The time to talk** about dating is not the first time your sons or daughters decide they want to go out; the time to talk is when your kids are leaving grade school to enter middle school, before they start showing interest in the opposite sex.

▶ **You still have** the right—and responsibility—to interview anyone before he dates your daughter, and make sure your son is capable to stand up to such scrutiny himself.

▶ **No matter how** mature your sons or daughters are, temptation is still the same. Do they have the wisdom to avoid situations that would allow the wrong thing to happen? If not, they are not yet ready to date , no matter how old they are.

> *I want you to be wise about what is good,*
> *and innocent about what is evil.*
>
> Romans 16:19, NIV

83

What should you teach them about love?

There is no question that falling in love is a pretty wonderful and miraculous thing. Though parents may not want their kids to grow up too quickly, at the same time they want them to find love in their lives and for that love to last a lifetime. How does a dad prepare them for what love is and, frankly, what love isn't? How does a dad help them separate what a media built on self-indulgence and consumerism says love is versus what the Creator of the universe says love is?

answer

When a person can use the same word to describe his attraction to NASCAR as he uses to describe how he feels about his wife, dog, children, the guy he likes to go fishing with, and a dessert, no wonder there is some confusion about what the word really means. While the Bible identifies different words for the kind of love you have for a friend, the romantic love you can feel for someone of the opposite sex, and the love of God shed abroad in our hearts, English rolls all of these into one. However, the distinctions are significant.

There is a fascination with the type of love that overwhelms people to the point of action. While this can be a good thing—such as when Jesus was moved with compassion to reach out and help others—today's society is more akin to using love as an excuse along the lines of "The devil made me do it."

God's love, on the other hand, has more to do with willing yourself to be a blessing no matter what it costs you. In a relationship and sexual context, God's love is the kind of love that keeps sex for marriage because it is what is best for both people. God's love is based on blessing, not getting. God's love is the type you need to teach your children about as well as show them every day.

worth thinking about

▶ **Respect and honor** for others are based on this type of love. Love practices good manners for the sake of others and goes to the trouble of learning how to be polite. Love is courteous.

▶ **Gossip powerfully** undermines what love is. Don't let your kids fall into the trap of talking about who is going out with whom and who did what on the weekends. The tongue can be bridled only by this kind of love.

▶ **Love is also** communicated in attitude and tone of voice. Walking in God's love should overpower teenage moodiness and angst.

> *Love is kind and patient, never jealous, boastful, proud, or rude. Love isn't selfish or quick tempered. It doesn't keep a record of wrongs that others do. Love rejoices in the truth, but not in evil. Love is always supportive, loyal, hopeful, and trusting.*
>
> 1 Corinthians 13:4–7, CEV

84

What should you teach them about money?

Teens are the largest consumer group in America today, spending as much as $50 billion a year. While more and more kids have disposable income, fewer and fewer of them have that money tied to any real-world expectations. Why is it that American society believes adolescents can run wild with cash, spending it on whatever they want, but that somehow when they go to college they will suddenly be wise with money?

answer

In order to set your kids up for success in life, one of the primary things you need to help them do is have a proper attitude toward money. The Bible says that the love of money is the root of all evil because greed is so blinding. How many kids stop to think about giving before they take the money they just got down to the store to buy a new video game or MP3 player? How many of them think, *Now this is extra money I don't really need—I should save at least half of it.* Or do they more likely think, *Aw, man, another hundred dollars and I could have had the eighty-gig iPod!*

If kids don't know the value of a dollar these days, it is because parents have not bothered to teach them or because parents have not let them learn it for themselves through working for it. Certainly kids should have an allowance to manage, but it should cover merely the basics. By the time your kids are entering their teen years, you should offer them other chances to make money by doing your chores around the house or working outside the home by mowing lawns or babysitting. Encourage your teen to take advantage of the many part-time and summer job opportunities available. With every dollar they make, they need to be giving at least 10 percent and saving another percentage for the future.

worth thinking about

▶ **Teens should have** giving goals as well as savings goals for things they want to buy. Do they have community projects they are financially supporting?

▶ **Is stewardship part** of the curriculum for your church's middle school ministry? Perhaps you can help them develop some lessons on it.

▶ **Don't rob your** child of opportunities to learn how to work. There are big jobs you can do better yourself, but if time is not an issue, let them plug away at one and see how they do.

> *There is an emotional and intellectual connection between work and money. . . . Life will not make "allowance" for you, but it will pay you what you earn. Work, get paid; don't work, don't get paid. Work, eat; don't work, don't eat. Even the Bible says this.*
>
> Dave Ramsey

85

question

Should they have a job?

As your kids reach the age of fourteen, they can get jobs for themselves, and at sixteen they can work at a coffee shop or restaurant. They can do yard work or babysit at even younger ages. However, is it better for them to work on their studies and their activities, or is it better for them to push a broom at the local corner market? Should you encourage your kids to get a summer job? What benefits are there for teens to work?

answer

Earning money and getting the sense of competence and responsibility that goes with a job well done is a great opportunity for a teenager. According to researchers, by age twelve about half of all kids have earned money doing some small jobs, and by the age of fifteen, nearly two-thirds have found some kind of part-time employment. Surprisingly, though, earning money doesn't directly correlate to being responsible with it—only about 11 percent of kids who earn money save anything for the future. The rest blow it on anything from designer clothes to the things their parents would never give them money for in the first place.

In other words, just getting a job will not necessarily teach kids to be more responsible, nor will it teach them the value of hard work. For teens who are not doing well in school but want to get a job in order to purchase the latest game system or some other distraction, a part-time job may be the last thing in the world you should let them apply for. For those teens who are already keeping up and have a balanced plan for the money they will earn, working a couple of hours right after school could help them learn even better time-management skills as well as help them pave the way toward exploring a career path for themselves.

worth thinking about

▶ **The better your** teen's relationship with money is, the better their relationship with a job will be. By the time they are able to get a job, they should understand the basics of keeping a budget and the value of giving.

▶ **A summer job** can be a great way to get your teens out from in front of the television and into the fresh air. Most parks departments have youth programs for maintaining trails and keeping public parks attractive and clean.

▶ **If your teen** is going to work, sit down with him or her and make a plan for what will happen with each paycheck.

> *Look at an ant. Watch it closely; let it teach you a thing or two. Nobody has to tell it what to do. All summer it stores up food; at harvest it stockpiles provisions. So how long are you going to laze around doing nothing?*
>
> Proverbs 6:6–9, THE MESSAGE

question

Should you debate your faith with your children?

answer

To know a truth well, one must have fought it out.

Novalis

question

▼

What about alcohol, drugs, and rock 'n' roll?

Statistics are staggering when it comes to adolescents who partake in risky behaviors while they are "partying" with friends. Teens who get involved with drugs and alcohol literally arrest the development of their brains as well as establish unhealthy patterns they will struggle against for the rest of their lives. How should you deal with issues surrounding drugs and alcohol with your teens?

answer

▼

You should deal with these issues head-on. Never forget that the word *parent* is a verb as well as a noun. Perhaps the toughest part of your being a father will be fixing solid limits for your teens and then holding those lines when they cross them. You need to be a solid, objective rock they can rely on to do what is right for them, even though they will probably never thank you for it until they are in their thirties.

First of all, draw your boundaries far from such activities. Never let your kids attend parties where there will not be adults you know and trust supervising and where you your-self will not be able to easily drop by. Keeping your kids out of compromising situations is something they won't necessarily understand, so hold the line firm. The more engaged you are with your kids, the more likely you are to be able to prevent your kids from falling into this trap.

At the same time, you need to realize that kids who do fall into this trap can get out, and that most have fallen in there by accident. Should your kids fall in with the wrong crowd and the wrong activities, be there to help them get out. Get professional help from intervention-ists, and turn your house into Fort Knox if necessary to help your kids overcome. This will be the toughest love you will ever have to contemplate.

worth thinking about

▶ By keeping your kids positively involved in clubs and activities working toward solid goals for the future, a great deal of stress can be prevented concerning the party scene. If they are friends with kids who don't use drugs and drink, peer pressure works in your favor.

▶ While your limits need to be strict, also help your kids to set limits of their own. If they are doing the right things only because you say so, what will they do when you are not around?

▶ Your own use of prescription drugs and alcohol sets an example for your kids in this area. The farther away you draw the line for yourself, the easier it will be to draw that line with your kids.

> *Run from temptations that capture young people. Always do the right thing. Be faithful, loving, and easy to get along with. Worship with people whose hearts are pure.*
> 2 Timothy 2:22, CEV

87

▼

What if they question their faith?

As teen brains are growing and changing and waking up to thinking for themselves, your kids will go through a process of analyzing everything you told them growing up and of seeing if it fits in with their new personal worldview. Will they decide that Jesus needs to go the way of Santa Claus, the Easter Bunny, and the Tooth Fairy, or that being a Christian and pursuing God is the only way to live? How should you handle it when they start to question the existence of God and the rightness of Christianity over other world religions?

answer

▼

If your kids never question their faith in their teen years in the safety of your home and protection of your church community, they are going to be in some trouble down the road. So don't only expect them to question what they believe, challenge them to do so. The more you talk over and debate why you believe what you believe with your kids as they are solidifying and taking ownership of their own beliefs, the better. And the more you have taught them to think and be intellectually honest in their arguments, the more effective they will be in keeping their faith through their college years and into adulthood.

about **being a great dad**

While it is important to keep such discussions open, never lose focus on the fact that Christianity is not so much a system of beliefs and philosophy for living as it is a relationship with God through His Son, Jesus Christ.

So take the time to put your kids on trial. Is there enough evidence in their lives to convict them of being a Christian? Do they know enough about what Christians believe and why they believe to be called members of the body of Christ?

worth thinking about

▶ **The scientific method**, by its very definition of proof through empirical physical evidence, cannot prove or disprove spiritual truth. Any proof of God must be more like deciding a court case than proving a scientific law.

▶ **There are really only** four options for who Jesus could have been: either (1) He is a legend, (2) He was crazy, (3) He lied about who He was, or (4) He is the Son of God. Looking at the evidence from this beginning can only logically lead to number 4 being true.

▶ **Check the apologetics** section of your local Christian bookstore for more detailed arguments to prove God exists and why Christianity is the only logical path to Him.

> *I personally have never heard a single individual—who has honestly considered the evidence— deny that Jesus Christ is the Son of God and the Savior of men. The evidence confirming the deity of the Lord Jesus Christ is overwhelmingly conclusive to any honest, objective seeker after truth.*
>
> Josh McDowell

question

▼

Is it important to eat dinner together?

Tutors, piano lessons, sports teams, club activities, parent-teacher nights, and Wednesday and Sunday night services—is that what most of your evenings before 8:00 p.m. look like? Finding a time for a family to regularly sit down to dinner together is more difficult now than ever. Is it really important for families to sit down to share a meal together, or can you replace this tradition of the past and find other times to communicate with your family?

answer

▼

Interestingly enough, researchers have found that families who eat dinner together experience a variety of benefits. First of all, those who eat together five or more times a week are less likely to take part in risky behaviors such as smoking, drinking, and drug use. They are also more likely to eat healthier meals and get better grades in school. Kids who eat regularly with their families also show a lower risk of depression and suicide. With so many good things happening as a result of one simple ritual, it makes sense to make it a big part of your family's routine.

Work to preserve this time by refusing to answer the telephone during dinner or refusing to eat with the television on. While this is an informal time, don't just bring the food to the table. Talk. Ask about subjects at school, discuss current events, share stories, and tell jokes. Ask about those your kids are in relationship with—friends, teachers, coaches, and so forth. Though you can use meals as a meeting time to discuss issues around the house, try to keep from doing this too often. Keep the time positive and informal, and allow your kids to steer the conversation for a time.

Family dinnertime should run together in your children's memories as a flowing river of conversation and laughter together. While it might be possible to accomplish all these things in other ways, there is certainly no simpler way to accomplish all of this in one simple activity. Make regular meals together a part of your family story.

worth thinking about

- ▶ As your kids get older, give them more opportunities to take part in preparing meals and being responsible for cooking regularly. Make cleanup a time together as well.

- ▶ Keep these times fun, the topics interesting, and avoid the clean-your-plate mentality.

- ▶ The meals themselves don't have to be elaborate affairs, though you want to keep them healthy and nutritious. Some families cook main dishes on the weekend for quick heat-ups for dinner during the week.

> Families that do have dinner together often are families whose parents are fully engaged with their kids.
> Richard Mulieri

question

▼

How do you make the most of a family vacation?

Vacations give you a chance to get away from the yard work, the household fix-it list, and the office to spend some extended time with your family. Depending on your budget, this could be touring art museums in Florence or camping at a nearby lake, but how do you keep these times memorable for your family? How much does the location matter? How much relaxation time should be worked in versus time for activities and sightseeing?

answer

▼

Too many dads plan elaborate vacations and try to fit in as many activities as possible, but they forget that the important aspect of family vacations is, in fact, family. Having the opportunity to take your kids to the Far East or Paris could well be the trip of a lifetime, and you may want to see as much as possible, but plan ahead of time what you will and won't do as a family. Then don't stress out if things don't go perfectly. Travel is an adventure, after all, especially travel to a foreign country. Mishaps should be part of the experience together rather than unexpected interruptions. Be thankful for the time away, and rejoice in whatever happens. Keeping your cool could make the difference between a trip that will be remembered with laughter and one your family would rather forget.

Should you take the action-packed adventure, don't neglect balancing it with another simple getaway just to hang out with your kids. Oddly enough, one common denominator of many great families is that they go camping together! Camping with your family provides a great opportunity to focus on one another because there are fewer distractions.

If you can, don't miss the opportunity to go on a missions trip as a family while your kids are in high school. It can be the adventure of a lifetime and inspire them to want to do the same with their kids down the road.

worth thinking about

▶ No matter the location, block out some unscheduled time in your itinerary. Also, let every family member pick an activity all of you will do together.

▶ While handheld computer consoles, laptops, and MP3 players can greatly ease a road trip, be sure to schedule some consistent "unplugged" time, even on the road. Turn the electronics off every couple of hours to play "I spy" games or sing crazy songs.

▶ Give everyone in the group a camera, even if it's a disposable one, and then put together journals of the trip with pictures developed along the way.

> *It is good to have an end to journey toward, but it is the journey that matters in the end.*
> Ursula K. Le Guin

90

question

▼

Do you treasure extended family and community?

Family memories are not just about your wife, your kids, and you. They are also about the extended family and the friends and neighbors who make up your community. Are you taking time to plan activities and vacations with these groups regularly? Does your church take time to socialize across generations, or does it plan events only by age levels? What about relatives you don't see much? Or how about your larger community and fairs and other festivals?

answer

▼

With the tendency of families to live farther and farther away from cousins and grandparents, making time to get together with extended family is more important than ever. Catching a plane to go to Grandma's for Thanksgiving or Christmas or getting the whole brood together at a national park for a week in the summer should be time to hear the stories and build the memories together that make people family. As you are planning the year and setting your budget, don't neglect to set aside time and resources to make these kinds of trips possible.

When you take trips to your parents' or your in-laws' house, make time to dig out the photo albums, carousels of slides, or eight millimeter or video footage and let the grandparents narrate. Ask questions about your grandparents and their siblings, and let your parents spin some yarns. Just because you aren't together doesn't mean your kids can't have regular interactions with their extended family. E-mail makes it easier than ever to stay in touch and keep everyone apprised of what is going on. Encourage your kids to share what they are doing and send pictures of their latest school play or club outing.

To find their way, kids need to learn the importance of older voices in their lives.

worth thinking about

▶ Grandparents are a powerful source of unconditional love and support for your kids that you cannot find anywhere else. They have a listening ear and perspective that give your kids context in the world. Make sure your kids benefit from them.

▶ Don't neglect your father's and mother's advice in raising your kids, either. When you stay close to your parents, it is easier for your kids to form strong bonds with them as well.

▶ Researchers have found that children with a good relationship with their grandparents have a better sense of community, family, and security.

> We don't accomplish anything in this world alone . . . and whatever happens is the result of the whole tapestry of one's life and all the weavings of individual threads from one to another that creates something.
>
> Sandra Day O'Connor

question

▼

How do you make holidays special?

Holidays can be a mixed bag of pressures to travel, spend time with extended family and in-laws, and over-tax your wallet and your beltline. Yet despite any of these drawbacks, holidays are the one set time in the yearly calendar when the world stops and gives you time to cherish your family. How do you keep these annual celebrations special and not arduous?

answer

▼

If you as the father take time out of your normal routine to make holidays fun, then holidays are sure to be memorable. Take the time to do special things for each of your family members, and the trend will quickly catch on. Though most holidays are about being home with your family, these breaks provide a great opportunity to get out of the house and do something different for a change. Check out your local paper for activities that fit the season, and surprise your family with turning off the television and having a night out for a concert in the park or a trip to the ice-skating rink. Chances are there are tons of local things to do, and most of them won't break your bank account. Remember to get involved with giving to others. Don't just contribute to food drives, but volunteer to deliver dinners to people's homes and go as a family.

Get together with your wife and talk about her family's holiday traditions as well as your own, and decide which ones you want to pass on to your kids. Make sure your traditions emphasize togetherness—decorate together, open gifts one at a time together, play games together, and so forth. Don't let the cooking be your wife's chore alone. Develop your own holiday special dishes and encourage your kids as they get older to go from helping to contributing dishes of their own.

Savor holidays together, and they can't help but be memorable and special. Whatever time you take planning and creating holiday fun will pay off a hundredfold.

worth thinking about

▶ **Always celebrate** the true meanings of holidays. Make the story of the birth of Jesus a big part of Christmas, and thankfulness the keynote of Thanksgiving. These "holy days" need to be remembered for more than football and turkey.

▶ **Make holidays** an excuse to meet the parents of your kids' friends. Let them plan the guest list and invite entire families.

▶ **Start a miniature** village display or a creative endeavor you can add to each year with something you make with your kids.

> *To many people holidays are not voyages of discovery, but a ritual of reassurance.*
> Philip Andrew Adams

question

▼

How are you sharing your family story?

What are your family roots? Do you know the history of your name and where your family was three hundred years ago? What are the stories you grew up on about your family that your parents and grandparents used to tell? How do they affect who you are today? Is yours a heritage that shows how people can change despite their past or one that inspires you toward great things? Where do your ancestors fit into the history your kids are learning at school?

answer

▼

Researching and reconstructing your family genealogy can be a great activity for spending time with your kids as well as for connecting them with extended family, culture, and history. It can start with something as simple as an expedition into your parents' attic to rummage through old chests, boxes of pictures, or paperwork. It can turn up journals that lead to hours of stepping into a very personal and interesting past with mysteries to be solved and insights to be discovered.

A great deal of personal history is lost because no one ever bothers to ask simple questions, questions about their grandparents' childhoods, how they met one another, or why they chose a certain profession. Teach your children about the art of interviewing and formulating questions. Exploring your heritage will also give your family an excuse to travel to destinations you might not otherwise have considered. Make it a point to follow your roots back to another continent or through a period of history your kids are studying at school.

Compiling such information can be a wonderful family hobby. Setting it up as a Web site can also connect family across distances as each part adds insight to the overall story. Great dads, after all, tend to be great storytellers, and what better stories to pass on than those about the exploits of your own relatives throughout history?

worth thinking about

▶ **Researching and reconstructing** your family genealogy is a great place to start. You can also use this information to create a family map showing where everyone has lived and traveled in their lifetimes.

▶ **During visits** with extended family, especially those that live far away, set up a time to get together and make a scrapbook page or two out of copies of things found in their home.

▶ **Put together DVDs** or scrapbooks of your findings with your kids and give them out as presents to relatives at Christmas or for an anniversary. Or you could put together a calendar of old family photos.

> *In every conceivable manner, the family is link to our past, bridge to our future.*
> Alex Haley

93

question

Do you serve your community together?

Stories have a tendency to happen no matter what you are doing, and serving others in hectic environments—whether it is working in a soup kitchen, running an activity with fellow church members for the children in your city, or building a church in a foreign country—leads to a lot of funny and memorable incidents. Do you take advantage of these opportunities to work together with your family serving others?

answer

Volunteering in your community with your family is a great way to come together as well as a great example for your kids of what life is really all about. One of the reasons Jesus told His disciples they needed to serve others was because service develops purpose in life. Service creates perspective and helps kids understand what is truly important. Working elbow-to-elbow with them serving others also shows them how much you value your community, as well as offers a chance to show them how rewarding working hard can be.

Volunteering in this fashion is a chance to showboat what being a great dad is all about. Your kids get to see you honestly caring for others and putting their needs before your own. They get to see your sense of humor in how you encourage others in the work, and they see you be one of the first to step up to do the hardest and least desirable jobs. They are able to observe your attitude when things don't go as planned and hear your wisdom as you press on anyway. They will see the respect that develops for you as you set the bar high for other volunteers to emulate.

By volunteering with your kids, you show them the power of one person to make a difference.

worth thinking about

▶ **Volunteering also** provides your kids with a practical way to develop their skills and talents in areas that will be valuable in the workplace down the road.

▶ **Is someone chronicling** the volunteer efforts your family is taking part in? When you head out to work in your community, don't forget your camera! Also carefully record your kids' work for future scholarship or job applications.

▶ **When you are** on the volunteer site, make a special effort to treat your kids just as you would any other volunteer. Let them report to the other people in charge and work alongside them.

> *Giving kids clothes and food is one thing but it's much more important to teach them that other people besides themselves are important, and that the best thing they can do with their lives is to use them in the service of other people.*
>
> Dolores Huerta

94

Should you be the family historian?

How are you recording your immediate family's story? Are you doing what most parents do: taking hundreds of pictures of your first child, dozens of the next, fewer still of the others? Do you have boxes of pictures, CDs, and video footage all tucked away in the attic next to your high school yearbooks? Or do you regard documenting your family's story as one of your hobbies and making things available and ready for when your grandchildren visit someday?

answer

Dads and cameras often seem to go together. While you can seem a nuisance buzzing around and continually clicking shots, you will be glad you did down the road for the memories you will have because of them. Don't just create boxes of photos or piles of CDs, though. Organize them into scrapbooks, and file them carefully for future project times together. Edit your raw video footage into fun films and DVDs that will entertain as well as tell your family story. As your kids move toward high school graduation, go back and edit together holiday footage into individual films that will show your kids growing up right before everyone's eyes.

Do you keep a journal? In these busy times, this may seem an impractical practice, but it is still a great way for you to chronicle your family story even if it is on a computer rather than in a leather-bound memoir. Though letter writing may also seem a lost art, are there collections of letters to your wife when you were courting that you could preserve somehow? Take the time on special occasions such as birthdays or graduations to write a letter to each of your kids letting them know how proud you are of them and who they are becoming. Make them worthy of your kids' hanging on to and rereading over and over as they grow older.

Be creative in how you record your family's story for your own enjoyment as well as for future generations'. It is a hobby that will pay rich dividends for generations to come.

worth thinking about

▶ **Make your picture** taking as invisible as possible. Try to limit the number of posed shots you set up and learn to be a master at taking candid shots.

▶ **Taking an annual** family portrait is a great gift for grandparents each year as well as a wonderful way to document your children's growing up for their kids.

▶ **A yearly newsletter** to family and friends is not all it can be without lots of pictures. It can be an easy way to stay in touch with extended family.

> *To live in hearts we leave behind is not to die.*
> Thomas Campbell

95

question

▼

Are you ready for when they leave home?

It is hard to accept, especially when your children are small, but the ultimate goal of having kids is that they would someday head out into the world on their own as competent adults who really don't need you anymore. As they grow older, are you truly preparing them for this day? Are you and your wife going to be ready to let them go and be confident the world will be a better place with them out in it?

answer

▼

One thing young fathers lack if they never have older dads to mentor them is a long-range view of what it means to raise a child from infanthood into adulthood. Everything a dad does today needs to be seasoned with the perspective of where he wants his children to be the day they graduate from high school. Over that span of time, your kids should actually grow increasingly more fun and interesting—not more and more of a problem— until the day you can look them in the eye and tell them you know they are ready to face the world on their own.

There will certainly be challenges and conflicts along the way. There will be times when it will tear your heart out as you sit on the sideline and let them solve issues for themselves you know you could easily solve for them. But if you did, you would rob them of a sense of responsibility, self-confidence, and accomplishment. There will be times you are convinced you really know nothing about being a dad, and then wonder how your kids grew to be so wise—and if you would be better off getting advice from them rather than being the one offering it.

No matter how old your children are, there will be a day when you set them free to blaze their own destinies. Determine that you will do what you need to today to prepare them for that certain tomorrow—and prepare your wife and yourself for it as well.

worth thinking about

▶ **Make a list** of what you want to do with your kids before they leave home. If you don't plan now, there will be too many things you'll regret not having done the day they leave home.

▶ **Let your relationship** with your kids change. You are no longer responsible for them; they are adults in the eyes of the law and responsible for themselves. Even if they are still in your home, hold them to that standard.

▶ **Take some time** with your wife to adjust, especially when your youngest child leaves home. Plan something fun for your first weeks "on your own."

> *Good parents give their children roots and wings. Roots to know where home is; wings to fly away and exercise what's been taught them.*
>
> Jonas Salk

How important is keeping a sense of humor?

Gentlemen, why don't you laugh? With the fearful strain that is upon me night and day, if I did not laugh, I should die.

Abraham Lincoln

question

▼

How do you stay on speed dial?

Just because they are out of your home and may have moved far away doesn't mean you don't want to hear from them regularly. Yet too often parents of adult children can't find a balance between keeping in touch and interfering with their kids' lives and relationships. As a great dad, you want to stay on speed dial for when they need advice or just want to talk, but what can you do to make sure they'll use it?

answer

▼

When your kids leave home for college or a career, first of all, be grateful. In a time when parents overall are doing less and less to help their children be capable, independent adults, more and more adult kids are not escaping the comfort of the couch in front of their parents' television set. Pat yourself on the back that they are moving out to be positive contributors to the world.

Of course, it won't take long for that to wear off and for you to miss them. It is great to stay in touch, but too much contact will just push them farther away. When they call, remember that your relationship has changed and you are no longer in charge of their lives. You are an ever-present support for them to do the right thing.

Listen when they talk, and don't offer opinions or judgments unless you are asked. And even then be hesitant to do more than express your confidence that they are capable of thinking for themselves. Ask them questions to help in the process. Kids often call home at this age for you to be a sounding board more than to tell them what to do.

Be interested in the events of their lives and share events from yours. What subjects are they taking? When is the term over? Keeping up with such regular, somewhat superficial happenings can keep you in touch and facilitate the harder calls when they need your ear for bigger decisions in their lives.

worth thinking about

▶ **When your kids** start their own families and have their own kids, keep track of their activities on a calendar. When you feel like calling, ask how one of those events or games went. Then encourage them to call you after the next one with an update.

▶ **E-mail is a** great tool for sending photos of what is happening with you as a gentle reminder to them to send their pictures to you.

▶ **Most cell phone** companies have free long-distance to certain numbers. Get service plans with your kids and urge them to use their cell phones just to catch up and let you know what is happening while they are waiting in lines.

> *A child becomes an adult when he realizes that he has a right not only to be right but also to be wrong.*
> Thomas S. Szasz

question

What if they don't ask for advice?

No matter how painful it is to you, and how easily it could have been avoided if "they had just listened," adult children learn many things the same way younger children do, by making their own mistakes and facing the consequences. Chances are if you trained them well when they were young—letting them experience their consequences when the stakes were low—they will be better off now. But what happens when you see your kids headed for disaster and they are not looking for your thoughts on the matter?

answer

It is tough to stand by and let your adult children make stupid decisions, but it is also a necessary part of helping them become competent, independent adults. If you still want to be accessible to them when they crash, then hold your tongue no matter how much you feel like telling them "I told you so." Perhaps it would help to remember that you made similar mistakes yourself when you left home. Share your own mistakes and laugh—and empathize—with them as you help them along the road to making repairs.

This, however, doesn't mean that you have to stand by silently as they sail their ship straight into an iceberg. Chances are if you did your job right when they were younger, they will still at least call you to let you know they are facing a big decision. Remember that as the father of an adult, you are no longer president of the board of directors. You are now a consultant asked to offer an opinion.

While you can use your own creativity to offer your thoughts through the back door, remember that once you have offered them, the decision is still theirs. Respect their competence to do the right thing—and don't forget you should continue to pray for them every day.

worth thinking about

▶ **Continue to set** firm limits with your kids, but now that they are adults this has to do more with you than with them. Refuse to tell them what to do or to feel guilty when they make mistakes.

▶ **If they ask** you directly what they should do, ask them, "Well, what were you considering doing?"

▶ **Mistakes are not** the end of the world. Help them consider worst-case scenarios, see the light at the end of the tunnel, and know that you are willing to walk along with them until they find it.

> *I have found the best way to give advice to your children is to find out what they want, and then advise them to do it.*
> Harry Truman

question

▼

What if they need money?

Your children have finally called after what has seemed forever to you, and before long you find out why—they need to borrow money. Figures. But what are you going to say? They left your house to be independent and self-reliant, but now they need money for a new car or for a business start-up. What happens when they fall behind on their payments? They call little enough now; what will it be like when they are really avoiding you?

answer

▼

One of the reasons you want to teach your kids about money while they are young is so that you don't end up in this situation. But if it happens, what are you going to do? For the right adult children, a loan from you can be just the key they need to launch the business or make the investment that will set them up for life. If you have the disposable cash that won't hurt if you don't get it back, and if you know your children to be fiscally responsible, loaning them money can be a tremendous blessing.

You need to know your kids, though, and for far too many, loaning money to adult children is asking for family strife. What do they need the money for? To pay off a loan, buy a car, get a new boat? Are they typically spenders or savers? Are you supplying all the money for the venture, or have they also set a good portion aside? You have to determine if loaning them this money will make them more responsible or less. If they have a track record of burning through their money or running up their credit cards, money from you now isn't likely to help. They are better off struggling through and learning how to get out on their own rather than having you bail them out.

Also, if you don't really have the money to lend and not getting it back could jeopardize your own plans for the future, then loaning them money is probably too risky. Be wise. Though saying no at the outset may be difficult, it is far better than trying to repair the relationship down the road after they have defaulted on paying you back.

worth thinking about

► **If you do decide** on giving your adult kids a loan, keep things businesslike, legal, and in writing. Make sure all the terms are specific and well understood.

► **If you have the** money, consider cosigning rather than giving a straight loan.

► **If you have** more than one child, don't stop treating them fairly. If you give one a loan, you should make the same available to them all, or else adjust your will accordingly.

> *Neither a borrower, nor a lender be;*
> *for loan oft loses both itself and friend.*
> William Shakespeare

99

question

▼

What if you don't like whom they're dating?

There is no question that the thrill of falling in love is intoxicating. It can blind your kids to flaws in the persons they are seeing regularly. What happens when they bring that special someone home to "meet the parents" and you think that the chosen one is a dud who will only cause heartache down the road? How do you politely tell your child to "dump the loser"? Or is this another area where you have to let your kids make their own mistakes?

answer

▼

Thinking about facing a situation like this is a great thing to do when your children are entering middle school. Resolve that you are going to raise them through their adolescent years so that this will never be something you have to face. Teach the skills they need to balance falling in love with finding someone who is compatible. Teach them to wait until marriage before they have sex. Teach them that sex creates a permanent bond with the other person and that premarital sex will cloud their judgment and feelings. Determine to be as preemptive as you can when your kids are younger, and hopefully this day will never come.

However, should this happen, you are right in assuming that marriage is too big a decision to stand by and let them make a mistake. While you still have to respect their independence, speak what you think and why you think it. Be specific, be kind, but also be direct.

Be as supportive as you can, but also someone who supports growth in both your child and the person he or she is dating. If they head for marriage together, strongly encourage quality premarital counseling with a minister whose judgment you trust. Chances are that all these steps will lead to a good result one way or another, and if your child decides to marry this person despite everything you have done, stand by to make it work.

worth thinking about

▶ **If the relationship** is getting more serious, consider spending some time with your daughter's fiancé—or have your wife spend time with your son's fiancée. Give them a chance to give you their perspective on the relationship.

▶ **Premarital counseling** can reduce the risk of divorce by 30 percent.

▶ **Don't get stuck** in your ways. It is still your child's life, and the only thing you have power over to change now is you. Seek advice and help from your minister on what you can do to make things smoother.

> *What you are as a single person, you will be as a married person, only to a greater degree. Any negative character trait will be intensified in a marriage relationship, because you will feel free to let your guard down.*
> Josh McDowell

question

How do you keep them coming for Christmas?

Your kids are grown and gone, but come holiday season the house feels empty without them. What can you do to make sure your kids and their new families feel welcome enough to keep them coming home for Thanksgiving, Christmas, and New Year's Day? How do you share them with your in-laws, and what do you do when you feel that you are not getting your equal time? How do you make being with you at least one holiday a year a tradition?

answer

Of course, the stronger your relationship was with your kids while they were growing up and the more fun you kept holidays when they were younger, the more your kids will want to share the magic of the holiday season at your house with their kids. While holidays are about family, they can also be about the tensions of having to get along with family. Are you a good host to your kids? If your kids' families and your in-laws live close enough, make room for the other sets of grandparents as well. Bringing everyone together rather than splitting holidays can be a more-the-merrier scenario, or your kids may choose to split the day between households and still spend it with both families.

If your kids live farther away, then there will be times when it is not practical or affordable for them to be with you over the holidays. Offer to go see them or to help pay for them to come see you. If you go there, remember to put on your best-guest-in-someone-else's-home behavior even though you are the patriarch. Don't insist on the same traditions you would in your own home, and focus on being a help rather than a burden.

You should never stop being a great dad to your kids, even when they have kids of their own. Your role will change a bit, but *love* is still spelled T-I-M-E—even if you have to split it between all of your children, your children-in-law, and your grandchildren.

worth thinking about

▶ **Continue traditions** you began with your children, but also allow room for your new son or daughter-in-law to incorporate ones from their families.

▶ **Whether you are** at your house or your kid's, find things to do throughout the season that are out of the house as well as in it. Don't let all of your activities be at the mall either. Think of other things to do together besides shop, watch football, and eat.

▶ **Look for holiday** opportunities to volunteer with your grandkids just as you did with your kids.

> *The best of all gifts around any Christmas tree: the presence of a happy family all wrapped up in each other.*
> Burton Hillis

Readers who enjoyed this
book will also enjoy

100 Answers to 100 Questions About Being a Great Mom

100 Answers to 100 Questions About God

100 Answers to 100 Questions About God's Promises

100 Answers to 100 Questions About Loving Your Husband

100 Answers to 100 Questions About Loving Your Wife

100 Answers to 100 Questions About Prayer

100 Answers to 100 Questions Every Graduate Should Know

100 Answers to 100 Questions to Ask Before You Say "I Do"